NON
OBVIOUS

Non-Obvious is a sharp, articulate, and immediately useful book about one of my favorite topics: the future. With actionable advice and entertaining stories, Rohit offers an essential guidebook to using the power of curation to understand and prepare for the future of business.

> — DANIEL H. PINK, best-selling author of *To Sell Is Human* and *When*

Shatter your magic crystal ball and toss out the tea leaves. In this book, Rohit shows us how and where to find the future trends that will shape your business, your brand, and even your own decision-making.

> — SALLY HOGSHEAD, best-selling author of *How the World Sees You*

There are very few books I read hoping that no one else around me will. They're the books that are so insightful, so thought provoking, and so illuminating that they provide a powerful competitive advantage. *Non-Obvious* is one of those. Pass on it at your own peril.

> — SHIV SINGH, former senior vice president/global brand, VISA; digital head PepsiCo; co-author of *Savvy: Navigating Fake Companies, Fake Leaders, and Fake News*

This is one of those rare books that deliver insights that are useful and help illuminate where business is going. It's a great read.

> — CHARLES DUHIGG, best-selling author of *The Power of Habit*

The best books approach their topic with a spirit of generosity. Rohit's new book offers insight into the business and cultural trends that matter, why they do, and what actions they might inspire. But more than that, it generously teaches how to develop your own process for evaluating the trends that matter and those that don't. Also, it's well-written, which makes it a joy and not a chore to read!

> — ANN HANDLEY, chief content officer, Marketing Profs

It doesn't take a crystal ball to predict that digital is the future. Rather than telling you what you already know, Rohit sets his sights on something much more important: helping you adopt a more curious and observant mindset to understand the world around you. If you believe in a lifetime of learning, read this book!

— JONATHAN BECHER, president, San Jose Sharks; former chief marketing officer, SAP

A lot of books promise to help you see things differently, but Rohit's book actually delivers. His insightful blend of visual thinking and business strategy shows you how to find meaningful patterns that others miss. A real mind-opener.

— SUNNI BROWN, author of *Gamestorming*

Non-Obvious is simple, elegant, and powerful: one of those intensely engaging books that I couldn't put down. Every year, I use the ideas in this book to help my team see new opportunities and out-think our competition.

— HOPE FRANK, chief marketing and digital officer + futurist

Rohit provides a gold mine of ideas and trends that will shape the future of marketing and product development. Read this book to get in front of the herd.

— GUY KAWASAKI, chief evangelist, Canva; author of *The Art of the Start, 2.0*

Lots of books tell you to "think different," but *Non-Obvious* is one of the few books that actually teaches you how to do it. Whether you are trying to persuade clients, motivate a team, or just impress a demanding boss, *Non-Obvious* can help you succeed. I've already purchased copies for my entire team.

— JOHN GERZEMA, best-selling author of *The Athena Doctrine*

Our industry is all about the future: the future of kids, the future of schools, the future of education. In the admissions office, the ability to recognize and leverage that future is an indispensable skill. In *Non-Obvious*, Rohit provides the tools we require to perform those functions with precision and get better at predicting what will be important tomorrow, based on improving our observations of today.

— **HEATHER HOERLE, executive director, Enrollment Management Association**

The insights in Rohit's *Non-Obvious* are an invaluable guide to understanding our customer's customer. His predictions are useful and highly anticipated within our group across the globe every year. As a B2B marketer and leader, this is one of my rare must-read recommendations for my entire team.

— **NAVEEN RAJDEV, former chief marketing officer, Wipro**

Non-Obvious is a powerhouse "must read" for corporate executives, marketers, and product and service developers. Rohit Bhargava provides valuable, entertaining, and easily understood sideways insights into critical trends shaping the near future. He lifts the lid on the myths surrounding the dark arts of trend prediction and offers practical guidance on how to spot, curate, and capitalize on Non-Obvious trends.

— **ROHIT TALWAR, global futurist and CEO, Fast Future Research**

Seeing things that others don't is perhaps the highest form of creativity that exists. Unlock the *Non-Obvious* approach, and you can write your ticket to success in any field.

— **JOHN JANTSCH, author of *Duct Tape Marketing* and *Duct Tape Selling***

Very few people understand the world of digital business better than Rohit, and I have introduced my clients to his ideas for years. His new book is a must-read resource for learning to see patterns, anticipate global trends, and think like a futurist every day!

— GERD LEONHARD, author and keynote speaker

I actually wish some of Rohit's predictions wouldn't come true ("Selfie Confidence"? Nooo!) . . . but usually they do. He's the best at this, and this book shows you why.

— SCOTT STRATTEN, four-time best-selling author, including the 2014 Sales Book of the Year, *UnSelling*

Artfully lacing stories together to pull out simple yet powerful trends, Rohit offers a blueprint for making trend identification a key component of your business strategy. The format of his book makes it easy for the novice to adopt these principles and for the expert to glean pearls of wisdom. While the title is *Non-Obvious*, your next step should be obvious: Read this book today!

— JOEY COLEMAN, chief experience composer, Design Symphony; author of *Never Lose a Customer Again*

Personality Not Included: Why Companies Lose Their Authenticity and How Great Brands Get It Back

Likeonomics: The Unexpected Truth Behind Earning Trust, Influencing Behavior, and Inspiring Action

ePatient: 15 Surprising Trends Changing Health Care (with co-author Fard Johnmar)

Always Eat Left-Handed: 15 Surprising Secrets for Killing It at Work and in Real Life

The Non-Obvious Guide to Marketing & Branding (Without a Big Budget)

The Non-Obvious Guide to Working Remotely (Without Getting Distracted, Lonely or Bored)

Beyond Diversity: 12 Non-Obvious Ways To Build a More Inclusive World (with co-author Jennifer Brown)

For the past 10 years, the Non-Obvious Trend Report has been one of the most widely read collections of future insights in the world, reaching well over 1 million readers. It's used annually by hundreds of global brand leaders.

This 10th Anniversary Edition features 10 new megatrends curated from thousands of stories, dozens of interviews and over 100 past trend predictions.

WINNER OF 20 INTERNATIONAL BOOK AWARDS, INCLUDING:

WINNER: Eric Hoffer Book Award (Business Book of the Year)

FINALIST: AMA-Leonard Berry Prize (American Marketing Association)

WINNER: Axiom Award (Gold Medal, Business Theory)

WINNER: Gold Stevie® – Book of the Year Award

FINALIST: The Montaigne Medal (Most Thought-Provoking Book)

WINNER: Soundview Best Business Book Award

WINNER: National Indie Excellence Award – Best Business Book

FINALIST: The Marshall McLuhan Award (Media Ecology Association)

OFFICIAL SELECTION: Gary's Book Club
(at the Consumer Electronics Show)

NON
OBVIOUS

HOW TO SEE WHAT OTHERS MISS
AND PREDICT THE FUTURE

MEGA
TRENDS

ROHIT BHARGAVA

FOUNDER + CHIEF TREND CURATOR,
NON-OBVIOUS COMPANY

IDEAPRESS
PUBLISHING

WASHINGTON, D.C.

IDEAPRESS
PUBLISHING

SECOND PRINTING

Published in the United States by Ideapress Publishing.
Ideapress Publishing | WWW.IDEAPRESSPUBLISHING.COM

Non-Obvious® is a registered trademark of the Influential Marketing Group.
All other trademarks are the property of their respective companies.

Cover Design by Jeff Miller
Cover Photo by Javier Pérez
Interior Design by Happenstance Type-O-Rama

Library of Congress Control Number: 2019917426.
ISBN: 978-1-94085-896-8 (Hardcover)
ISBN: 978-1-64487-002-8 (Paperback)

SPECIAL SALES
Ideapress books are available at a special discount for bulk purchases for
sales promotions or corporate training programs. Special editions, including personalized covers and custom forewords, are also available. For more
details, email info@ideapresspublishing.com or contact the author directly.

To my parents — for always giving me

a chance to see the world in my own way . . .

even if it wasn't always non-obvious.

CONTENTS

PART I

The Art of Non-Obvious Thinking

INTRODUCTION

"I am not a speed reader. I am a speed understander."

— ISAAC ASIMOV, author, historian, and biochemist

THE YEAR IS 1962, and a man named Robert Townsend has just fired his entire advertising department.

The company he recently took over hasn't been profitable in more than a decade and if he expects to reverse its fortune, he needs a big idea — but he doesn't have a big budget. In desperation, he sends a short brief to a handful of creative directors from the hottest ad agencies in New York, asking a single impossible question: "How do we get five million dollars of advertising for one million dollars?"

One agency responds with an unusual proposition. Bill Bernbach, founder of renowned ad giant Doyle Dane Bernbach (DDB), asks for ninety days to study the business and agrees to take the job on one condition: Townsend must promise to run any advertising idea proposed by DDB exactly as written without question.

He agrees.

DDB starts by commissioning a series of focus groups, but the results are disheartening. The brand is a distant second place behind the dominant industry leader and there isn't much hope of closing the gap. Tasked with finding some insight they might use to build a campaign, an unknown copywriter named Paula Green has an unusual idea.

As a rare female copywriter during the notoriously male-dominated golden era of advertising, Green is already accustomed to bringing a different perspective to her work. Inspired by something she hears employees say during the focus groups, she writes a brutally honest new campaign tagline: *"Avis — We're only No. 2. We try harder."*

Townsend is skeptical at first.

Why would any brand spend money to advertise being second best — especially one struggling as badly as his? But true to his word, he reluctantly approves the campaign as written.

The ads are an instant hit. Less than 12 months after the campaign starts, Avis goes from losing $3.2 million annually to earning $1.2 million. Within a matter of years, some predict the campaign will soon need an update because Avis will no longer be number two. The tagline becomes a rallying cry for employees as well, serving as a manifesto they would use continually for the next fifty years. Today it is widely regarded as one of the best advertising campaigns ever.

Why did it become so iconic?

The question has inspired decades of debate. Some suggest it was the result of a unique trusted relationship between the brand and its agency. Others believe it was the humility in the tagline that helped humanize Avis and inspired their employees to indeed try harder in every customer interaction. Leadership experts instead credit Townsend's renowned people-first management style.

Green herself suggested the campaign worked because it "went against the notion that you had to brag." She also noted, with some irony, that as a woman in advertising, having to try harder was "somewhat the story of [her] life."

Her comment suggests there may be an overlooked detail in this story. Of the dozens of people involved in focus groups, everyone failed to appreciate the significance of that one employee's comment about trying harder.

Everyone but Paula Green, the one person who saw what everyone else missed.

WHY I WROTE THIS BOOK

This is a book about what it takes to see what no one else sees.

This skill is often described as creativity, and we live in a world that celebrates it. But finding the solution to a particularly tricky problem or discovering a world changing idea takes more than creativity—a fact I discovered one fateful day nearly two decades ago while sitting across the table from a man waiting to be inspired by anyone but me.

It is 2001 and I have been working in advertising for less than a year. It's long enough to understand the hierarchy. There are the *creatives*—who have cool titles like "Wizard of Lightbulb Moments"—and there are the rest of us.

I am not a creative.

We're sitting in a conference room on the top floor of an office building overlooking Darling Harbor in Sydney, outfitted with an enormous table made of Tasmanian oak (as our clients make a point of telling us). It is an intentionally intimidating setup.

As we present our epic game changing campaign idea, I can't help feeling quietly relieved that no one expects me to say anything. At first the presentation seems to go well. Unfortunately, as our pitch wraps up our client asks the one question we were not expecting: "What else you got?"

This is not good.

We had spent two months preparing for this meeting and our creative team was so convinced it was a winner, that they hadn't even brought a backup idea.

Our response to his question was truly terrible. Silence.

I slowly realized that the only person who could remember those abandoned ideas was the junior member of the team who had taken notes in all the meetings: me. Summoning my courage, I broke the silence and spoke up. It was a moment that would change my career . . . though not perhaps in the way you might imagine.

I did not pull a million-dollar idea out of my head. In fact, the truth is I don't remember what I said. But I do remember how I *felt*.

It was my first taste of what it meant to be on the other side, and I was hooked. I wanted to have that feeling again.

Unfortunately, creativity still wasn't my job. And judging from our failed client encounter, maybe creativity wasn't even the right word to describe what our clients actually wanted anyway.

Around that time I found inspiration in the words of an author who was once asked by novelist Kurt Vonnegut what it felt like to be "the man who knows everything."

WHY SPEED READING DOESN'T MATTER

Isaac Asimov has earned that reputation by writing nearly 500 books in his prolific lifetime. He is most widely known for his ground-breaking work in science fiction, but he also wrote everything from an illustrated children's guide to dinosaurs to a comprehensive two-volume guide to The Bible.

How could one man have interests and skills so varied that he could write and publish an average of more than ten books every year? Asimov credited his creative thinking to his legendary appetite for reading and learning about everything he could from a young age.

"I am not a speed reader," he once said. "I am a speed understander." *What if you could be a speed understander too?*

It's hard to imagine following Asimov's recipe for understanding in today's world. We are inundated by content, and most of it is not good. It has become nearly impossible to separate the bullshit from the believable. Digital tools have made it easy for everyone to share ideas, even if they are one-dimensional or idiotic. Yet bullshit, no matter how well packaged and easily distributed, remains bullshit.

To face this landslide of bad content, we are increasingly relying on a combination of algorithms and one-dimensional opinions shared on social media to help us filter the noise. And we've pioneered new methods of skimming out of sheer desperation. We watch television at accelerated speed, use speed-reading apps that flash a single word at a time, and turn to productivity gurus specializing in "time hacking."

None of these solutions work for long.

The problem is that expecting to get smarter from processing content faster is a bit like entering a speed-eating contest to enjoy a good meal. Eating 26 hot dogs in 60 seconds might satisfy your hunger, but you're likely to feel sick afterwards.

You can't understand the world better simply by reading about it as much as possible. You do so by being intentional about what you pay attention to in the first place. What if you could become a life-long learner, curious about the world and able to see, understand, and expect things others miss? What if you could use that skill to understand patterns, spot intersections and see around the corner to develop an observation of what the future might hold? And what if, once you put all the pieces together, you could actually learn to predict the future?

You can, and the ambitious aim of this book is to teach you how to do it. I call my approach *Non-Obvious Thinking*, and it can change your life. It changed mine, as I realized years ago after spending a memorable afternoon in Norway surrounded by 50,000 bottles of alcohol that I couldn't drink.

WHAT I LEARNED FROM A NORWEGIAN BILLIONAIRE

Christian Ringnes is one of the richest men in Scandinavia. A flamboyant businessman and art collector, he made his fortune in real estate and was the driving force and financier behind the critically acclaimed Ekeberg Sculpture Park in Oslo, Norway. Yet his legacy may come from a far quirkier accomplishment: amassing one of the largest independent collections of miniature liquor bottles in the world.

His decades-long obsession eventually ran into an insurmountable opponent: his wife, Denise. Tired of the clutter, she offered him an ultimatum: Find something to do with the more than 52,000 bottles he had amassed or start selling them. Like any other avid collector, Ringnes couldn't bear the thought of parting with his beloved bottles, so he did exactly what you might expect a

Norwegian real estate tycoon to do: he commissioned a museum for his bottles.

Today his Mini Bottle Gallery is one of the world's top weird museum destinations, routinely featured in offbeat travel guides. When I took a tour of the gallery, I was fascinated by how it was organized. Every room featured bottles grouped into quirky themes ranging from a "Room of Sin" inspired by a brothel to a "Horror Room" featuring liquor bottles with trapped objects such as mice or worms floating inside.

More important, like other well-crafted museum experiences, the Mini Bottle Gallery is carefully curated. Only about 20 percent of Ringnes' collection is on display at any one time. This thoughtful selection creates meaning for the entire gallery because each room tells a story, and those stories bring the experience to life.

As I walked out of the museum that evening, I realized just how important this idea of curation might be to my own work. What if the secret to having better ideas that clients loved was to get better at *curating* them before I needed them?

HOW I BECAME AN IDEA CURATOR

Back in the middle of 2005, I was part of a team tasked with starting what would become one of the largest and most successful social media teams in the world. At that time, social media basically meant blogging, so our services involved helping large brands find ways to engage bloggers directly.

Writing a blog seemed easy, so I decided to start one myself. My first few posts came easily, but then I ran out of ideas.

How was I going to keep my hastily created blog constantly updated with new stories when I already had a full-time day job? I needed a better method for collecting ideas.

I started seeking ideas everywhere. At first, I gathered them by emailing links of stories to myself. I scribbled possible blog topics on scraps of paper. I saved quotes from books and ripped pages out of magazines. As my collection of potential topics grew, I started saving them in a simple yellow folder with *Ideas* scrawled on the tab.

Soon worn from use, it was held together at its badly ripped seam by a tired piece of duct tape.

It worked, and I now had plenty of inspiration for what to write about. I did that religiously for four years, at times posting a new article every day.

During that time, I wrote more than a thousand articles and built a readership of hundreds of thousands of people. The blog won several awards, helped grow my network, and eventually helped me land a deal with McGraw-Hill to publish my first book, *Personality Not Included*, in 2008.

Two years later, I did something that would shape the next decade of my life.

THE BIRTH OF THE *NON-OBVIOUS TREND REPORT*

Near the end of 2010, I was reading article after article about trends for the coming year. Almost all of them were lazy, uninformed, or self-serving declarations of the obvious. According to one, the hottest trend of the year would be the iPhone 4. Another article suggested that "more people would express themselves on social media." Yet another predicted that 2011 would be the Year of Drones. Not surprisingly, that one was written by the CEO of a company that made drones.

These weren't trends — they were profoundly obvious observations of the world.

At best they were wishful thinking, and at worst they were veiled pitches for products or services hoping to profit from being considered trendy. In a frustrated bid to do better, I published my own list of 15 trends and called it the *Non-Obvious Trend Report*, named as a not-so-subtle criticism of all the blatantly obvious trend predictions I had read.

The report went viral as hundreds of thousands of people read and shared it.

Over the next five years, what started as a 20 page PowerPoint presentation shared online evolved into a robust annual trend report with hundreds of pages of research, interviews, panels and eventually, in 2015, a bestselling print edition of the book you now hold in your hands.

Along the way, I left my job at Ogilvy, became an entrepreneur, spoke on some of the biggest stages in the world and published a new annual edition of the book with updated trends every January.

Now, ten years and nine editions later, my library of non-obvious trends has grown to more than a hundred predictions. The books have been translated into eight languages, earned nine prestigious international book awards, and reached well over a million readers. They also have led people to label me with a title I always struggled to embrace: a futurist.

WHY I AM A RELUCTANT FUTURIST

I am inspired by futurists who look at the world today and anticipate what will come. Reading *The Next 100 Years* by leading futurist George Friedman, for example, is like being engrossed in both a wonderful work of science fiction and a prescient description of potential reality. The year 2060 indeed might begin the "Golden Decade," as he predicts. *That* is how futurists think.

In comparison, my team and I research trends to help brands and leaders understand the accelerating present and act on that knowledge today. That's why "futurist" always felt like an overstate-ment to me.

In past interviews, I have described myself instead as a "near futur-ist." My lens typically focuses on trends that are affecting our behavior or beliefs right now. However, that doesn't mean my annual trend predictions expire; instead, if well predicted, they become more obvi-ous over time.

HOW TO READ THIS BOOK

After a decade of making predictions, my team and I have seen some trends evolve into broader cultural or behavioral shifts while others have faded in significance.

In this tenth anniversary edition of *Non-Obvious*, we will take a look at the past decade of research and incorporate the most signif-icant trends and stories while offering a broader context around the urgent need for more non-obvious thinkers in the world.

In Part 1, you will discover the five key mindsets required for being a non-obvious thinker, followed by a detailed look at my signature Haystack Method for curating trends and techniques for putting insights into action.

Part 2 of the book features predictions of ten powerful mega-trends that will shape the coming decade, along with implications for culture, business, careers, and humanity. Each chapter also explores the potential implications each of the megatrends are likely to have in our world.

Finally, Part 3 includes a candid review of every previously pre-dicted trend from the past nine years, along with a curated rating of how each one fared over time and the fascinating backstory of how the report itself evolved from year to year.

As you'll learn throughout this book, the benefits of learning to be a *non-obvious thinker* go far beyond just being able to identify trends. Seeing the non-obvious makes you more open minded to change and can help you disrupt instead of getting disrupted.

Non-obvious thinking can make you the most creative person in any room, no matter what your business card says and help solve your biggest problems. Most importantly, non-obvious thinking can help you anticipate, predict and win the future.

Ultimately the biggest lesson may be that you don't need to be a speed reader to win the future. Being a speed understander is a far worthier aspiration. It's my hope that this book will help you get there.

01 THE 5 MINDSETS OF NON-OBVIOUS THINKERS

"I have studied thousands of people. . . and it's breathtaking how many reject an opportunity to learn."

—CAROL DWECK, author of *Mindset*

I AM SITTING IN A CLASSROOM WITH twenty-five nervous students.

I'll be their professor for a ten-week course at Georgetown University focused on public speaking and being more persuasive. As my new students introduce themselves, more than half start by declaring that they are not very good at public speaking. For the next several years, every class begins the same way.

As I reviewed my students' progress throughout the course year after year, a pattern emerged. The students who introduce themselves as poor speakers end up making less progress than the ones who don't. On some level, this makes sense. Some people are naturally better public speakers than others, right?

What surprised me, though, was that this divide rarely related to who was the better speaker. In fact, some students routinely overrated their own skills while others seemed to hold themselves and their own talent back. Success wasn't determined by natural ability. Something else was happening.

The work of renowned Stanford psychology professor Carol Dweck offers one possible explanation. Dweck spent decades working with elementary school students, interviewing professional athletes, and studying business leaders to discover why some people managed to fulfill their potential while others failed.

Her landmark conclusion was that it all came down to individual mindset.

Most people have either a growth mindset or a fixed mindset, Dweck suggested. People with fixed mindsets believe that their skills and abilities are set. They see themselves as being either good or bad at something and tend to focus their efforts on tasks and careers where they feel they have a natural ability.

People with growth mindsets believe that success is the result of learning, hard work, and determination. They think that they can achieve their true potential through effort. As a result, they thrive on challenges and often have a passion for learning. They are also more likely to treat failure as "a parking ticket, not a car wreck." They're more resilient, have more self-confidence, and tend to be happier.

Engaging in non-obvious thinking starts with adopting a growth mindset. Yet mindset alone does not explain why some people are able to see what others miss while others remain stuck doing things the way they always have.

My obsession with non-obvious thinking during the past decade led me to study the processes of hundreds of thinkers, business leaders, and authors. Many of them were the leaders behind industry-changing innovations, and all of them were wildly successful. Beyond having a growth mindset, I uncovered five additional mindsets that these non-obvious thinkers had adopted to propel themselves and their organizations toward the future faster than others.

THE FIVE MINDSETS OF NON-OBVIOUS THINKERS

BE OBSERVANT

See what others miss.

BE CURIOUS

Always ask why.

BE FICKLE

Learn to move on.

BE THOUGHTFUL

Take time to think.

BE ELEGANT

Craft beautiful ideas.

Be Observant

Pay attention to the world, and train yourself to notice the details that others miss.

One day I was standing on a jet bridge waiting for my gate-checked carry-on bag to be delivered. The bags that came up first all seemed to have a yellow handle cover, so I asked a fellow traveler about it. He told me that United Airlines issues those covers to fliers with top-tier status. They indicate to the ground staff that those bags should be brought up first. I realized that I had a cover at home but had never thought to put it on my bag because I hadn't realized its significance.

The next week I started using it, and as expected, my luggage arrived first along with those of other frequent travelers. Did those few saved minutes change my life? Of course not, but they did make my experience that day a little bit better. Added up over dozens of flights, the time saved becomes significant.

Being observant isn't simply about seeing the big things. It's also about training yourself to pay attention to the little things. What do you see about a situation that other people are missing? What do the details you notice teach you about people, processes, and companies that you didn't know before? And how can you use that knowledge to win — even if that victory is something as small as getting your luggage a little bit faster than everyone else?

WATCH A VIDEO ABOUT THIS HABIT:
www.nonobvious.com/megatrends/resources

THREE WAYS TO BECOME MORE OBSERVANT

 EXPLAIN THE WORLD TO CHILDREN.
One of the best ways to hone your observation skills is to explain the world around you to children. For example, when one of my kids asked me recently why construction vehicles and traffic signs are yellow, but most cars aren't, it forced me to think about something I might never have considered. (Answer: Yellow is more visible from a distance, and in American culture, it is recognized as a color associated with messages of "caution" or "alert.")

 WATCH PROCESSES IN ACTION.
Many interactions in life, from how the barista makes your coffee to who gets an upgrade on a flight, are controlled by some mysterious system. The next time you interact with a company or person in a profession or environment different from yours, pay attention to the details. What processes do they engage in? How does each person you interact with handle the process differently? When you notice these processes instead of ignoring them, you literally can see what everyone else misses.

 PUT YOUR DEVICES AWAY.
Our devices excel at keeping us from seeing the world around us. Instead of navigating daily tasks such as walking down the street or taking the subway with your eyes fixed on your phone, try putting it away and looking around. Look for interesting things, observe people's body language, or start a conversation with a stranger.

Be Curious

Ask questions, invest in learning, and approach unfamiliar situations with a sense of wonder.

Bjarni Herjulfsson could have been one of the most famous explorers in the history of the world. Instead, his life has been largely forgotten.

In A.D. 986, Herjulfsson set off from Norway on a voyage to find Greenland. Blown off course by a storm, his ship became the first European vessel in recorded history to see North America. Despite his crew's pleas to stop and explore, Herjulfsson guided his ship back on course and eventually found Greenland. Years later, he told this tale to a friend named Leif Erikson, who, inspired by Herjulfsson's adventure, purchased his ship and undertook the journey himself.

Erikson is widely remembered as the first European to land in North America — nearly 500 years before Christopher Columbus landed in the Bahamas and supposedly discovered America. Herjulfsson, by contrast, has been forgotten. His story offers a vivid reminder of why curiosity matters: It's a prerequisite to discovery.

We humans are naturally curious, but often bury our curiosity because it can seem like a distraction. It is easier to move on than to stop and explore something more deeply. Even our own knowledge can hold us back. The more we know about a topic, for example, the more difficult it becomes to think outside our expertise and broaden our view. Psychologists describe this phenomenon as the "curse of knowledge."

Here are some methods to rekindle your curiosity and break this curse.

THREE WAYS TO BECOME MORE CURIOUS

 CONSUME "BRAINFUL MEDIA."
We are surrounded with brainless content—from gossip blogs to reality shows featuring unlikable people doing unlikable things. Although brainless content can be addictively entertaining, it encourages passivity, not curiosity. Instead, consume content and experiences that fuel your curiosity and make you think. Watch an engaging TED Talk, read a book on a topic you know little about, or attend a lecture on an unusual topic.

 READ UNFAMILIAR MAGAZINES.
One of my favorite ways to see the world through someone else's eyes is to read magazines that are not targeted at me or describing the culture I live in. For example, *Modern Farmer*, *Pacific Standard*, and *Monocle* are three vastly different magazines. Simply flipping through the stories, advertisements, and imagery of magazines like these takes me outside my own world (and geography) instantly and more easily than almost any other 10-minute activity.

 ASK QUESTIONS CONSTANTLY.
A few years ago, I was invited to deliver a talk at an event for the paint industry. I arrived early, wandered around the exhibit hall and asked many questions. In 30 minutes, I learned how paint is mixed, why there is an industry debate about the virtues of all-plastic cans versus steel ones, and what impact computerized color-matching systems had on sales. I have had similar experiences and conversations with thousands of professionals across dozens of industries. The result is that I know a little bit about so many different groups that I'm confident I can make any talk relevant for any audience. My curiosity has prepared me to succeed working in any industry.

NON-OBVIOUS MINDSET #3:

Be Fickle

Save interesting ideas for later consumption without overanalyzing them in the moment.

Being fickle usually isn't seen as a good thing. When it comes to encountering new ideas, though, I have found an underappreciated upside to learning how to be purposefully fickle. To illustrate why this works, consider how frequent-flier miles work. You don't take a flight, collect a few thousand miles, and turn around immediately and try to use them.

Instead, you collect those miles until you finally accrue enough to go somewhere interesting. *What if you could collect ideas the way most of us collect frequent-flier miles?*

The key to doing so is avoiding the temptation to fixate on assigning meaning to every idea instantly. I realize that on the surface, this may seem counterintuitive. After all, why wouldn't you take the time to analyze a great idea and explore it right away?

Any experienced facilitator or creative coach will tell you that the best way to kill the flow of a brainstorming session is to dwell on individual ideas. Ideation and analysis need a buffer of time between them for either to be effective. Often the meaning of ideas and the connections among them surface only after setting the ideas aside. Analyzing them later can give you more ideas and perspectives that enable you to see the connections more deeply.

When you read a book that had sat on your bookshelf for months or years, you experienced the hidden power of being fickle. When you bought the book, it might not have been the ideal time for you to read it. Having it on your shelf allows you to turn to it later, when you are ready to discover it.

Being fickle isn't about abandoning ideas too quickly or being unable to focus. It's about freeing yourself from the pressure to recognize connections among ideas immediately and making it easier to return to a collection of ideas to analyze them later.

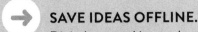 **SAVE IDEAS OFFLINE.**
Digital note-taking tools can be great at saving information, but most tend to prioritize recently added content and bury the rest. While I do use note-taking apps on my phone, I tear stories out of magazines and put them all in an ideas folder that sits on my desk. Saving ideas offline enables me to give each one equal weight, no matter when I saved it. Having them in physical form also enables me to spread them out later—a key element of the Haystack Method that you'll learn in Chapter 3.

SET YOURSELF A TIME LIMIT.
To avoid the temptation to overanalyze an idea, try using a timer to limit how much time you spend on it. This technique can help clear your mind and enable you to evaluate more quickly whether an idea is worth saving for closer examination later.

TAKE SHORTER NOTES.
When I gather these articles and stories throughout the year, I usually jot down a few words to remind me why I found something interesting. I also use colored tab stickers when reading books to mark sections of interest. Whenever possible, I use a Sharpie marker to do this because the thicker lettering stands out and forces me to make only the most useful observations in the moment.

Be Thoughtful

Take time to develop a meaningful point of view, and consider alternative viewpoints.

The Internet is sadly filled with useless, biased, half-thought-out comments and uninformed opinions.

Being thoughtful is harder to do when the priority seems to be responding quickly, regardless of what you have to say. When having a discussion with friends or colleagues, responding to an email or article in a blog, or even interacting with a store clerk or service representative, many of us rush to say something simply to fill the silence or to speak up before anyone else does.

To be more thoughtful, we need to remind ourselves to take a moment and consider the divergent thoughts of those around us, particularly those who may not think the same way we do. We need to be intentional when reading, sometimes seeking out several sources for the same story. When I see how different people and often sources from different countries report on the same thing, for example, I build a wider perspective for myself.

THREE WAYS TO BECOME MORE THOUGHTFUL

 WAIT A MOMENT.
Whether you are interacting online or in person, taking the time to think about what you want to say always pays off. Not only will you say what you really mean, but you'll avoid making a gaffe because you haven't considered how others might misinterpret your thoughts.

 WRITE. THEN REWRITE.
The most talented writers take time to edit or entirely rewrite their work rather than share the first draft. The process of self-editing and rewriting can be time-consuming (I know!). If you feel that way, remember that the most engaging form of writing is dialogue, so when in doubt, write it as you would say it.

 EMBRACE THE PAUSES.
As a speaker, I needed years of practice before I was comfortable with silence. It's not easy. When you use pauses effectively, you emphasize the points you really want people to hear and give yourself time to articulate what you want to say in a conversation or from the front of the room if you're presenting to a group. Thoughtful, persuasive people aren't afraid of silence.

Be Elegant

Describe ideas or insights in more beautiful, deliberate, simple, and understandable ways.

Jeff Karp is a scientist inspired by elegance and jellyfish. A bioengineer at Brigham and Women's Hospital in Boston and professor of medicine at Harvard Medical School, Karp focuses his research on using bio-inspiration from nature to develop new solutions for all types of medical challenges. His eponymous Karp Lab has developed such innovations as a device for capturing circulating tumor cells in cancer patients, inspired by jellyfish tentacles, as well as better surgical staples, inspired by porcupine quills.

Although Karp's research focuses on finding inspiration in nature's elegance, you can apply the same principle to how you describe ideas. Simplicity is fundamental to being elegant in how we express ourselves . When you eliminate unnecessary words, you can distill your ideas and make them easier to understand.

THREE WAYS TO THINK MORE ELEGANTLY

 KEEP IT SHORT.
Simplicity goes hand in hand with elegance. When it comes to expressing your ideas, this usually means using as few words as possible. It is also a well-known marker of expertise that when you truly understand something, you can explain it to a layperson without dumbing it down.

 USE POETIC LANGUAGE.
Poets use metaphors, imagery, alliteration, and other tools to express emotion and meaning in their writing. What can you do to use more provocative language and avoid clichés? Everything doesn't need to be "great" or "awesome." Why not describe it as breathtaking or miraculous, or badass, or formidable? Thanks to the Internet, better words are at your fingertips. Choose to seek them out.

 BREAK IT INTO PIECES.
Breaking down an argument or complex situation into its relevant components helps you understand it and explain it to others. Pilots, for example, use detailed checklists to ensure they don't miss a step before taking off, an elegant solution for making the complex more understandable.

PUTTING THE HABITS INTO ACTION

These five key mindsets can help you think differently and escape lazy thinking that leads to obvious ideas. By adopting them, you'll become better at seeing the connections among the stories you read, the media you watch or hear, and the conversations you have. You'll find yourself having more insights than your peers and seeing what others miss.

Once you get in the habit of using the five mindsets, you'll be ready to take your non-obvious thinking to the next level: identifying interesting ideas and patterns and curating them into insights that can help you win the future. In the next chapter, you will learn how, using a process I call the Haystack Method.

02 THE HAYSTACK METHOD FOR CURATING NON-OBVIOUS IDEAS

"The most reliable way to anticipate the future is to understand the present."

— JOHN NAISBITT, futurist and author of *Megatrends*

IN 1982, THE BOOK *MEGATRENDS* changed the way governments, businesses, and people thought about the future. As you may have guessed, it was an inspiration for me as well even though the first time I read it was nearly 25 years after its initial publishing.

The author, John Naisbitt, was one of the first to predict humanity's evolution from an industrial society to an information society, and he did so more than a decade before the advent of the Internet. He also predicted the shift from hierarchies to networks and the rise of our global economy. Despite the book's unapologetic American-style optimism, most of the 10 major shifts Naisbitt described were so far ahead of their time that when the book was first released, one reviewer glowingly called it "the next best thing to a crystal ball." With more than 14 million copies sold worldwide, it's still the single best-selling book about the future published in the past 40 years.

Naisbitt is famous for believing in the power of observation and curiosity. In interviews, friends and family often describe him as having a "boundless curiosity about people, cultures, and organizations," even noting that he has a habit of scanning "hundreds of newspapers and magazines, from *Scientific American* to *Tricycle*, a Buddhism magazine," in search of new ideas.

At 90 years old, Naisbitt still is a collector of ideas. As he often explained, if you want to get better at anticipating the future, start by getting better at understanding the present.

Unfortunately, understanding the present isn't easy. The big picture is hard to see when everyone in your circle is trying to sell you the nicest frame to put around it. When thinking about the future, many people encounter the pitfall of describing something that is ultimately transient and meaningless.

The problem is, most people don't know what a trend is or isn't. Let's start with a definition: ***A trend is a curated observation of the accelerating present.***

HOW DO TRENDS AND FADS DIFFER?

Trends can help us anticipate the future and change what we do and think. The problem is that many so-called trends are actually short-lived fads. The line between trends and fads can be blurry. Although some trends may seem to spotlight a currently popular story or cultural event, they typically describe behaviors and beliefs that develop over time. Fads describe something that's briefly popular but doesn't last. Great trends reflect a moment in time, but that moment is never fleeting, and the basic idea is more elevated.

Good trends always focus on the shift in an underlying human behavior or belief. They don't describe a single interesting story or a hot new product or industry.

Here's an example. A few years ago, someone asked whether I considered the rise of 3D printing to be a trend. I replied that I did not, but I viewed the rise of the *maker movement* of people who want to create something on their own (which 3D printing certainly enables) was a trend worth watching.

One term commonly heard in the art of predicting the future is *trend spotting*. The term suggests that trends sit out in plain sight, ready to be observed and cataloged like avian species for birdwatchers. Trend spotters tend to focus on finding interesting stories or anything else that stands out.

Trend spotting isn't the same as identifying actual trends. When you focus on spotting stories that stand out, you gravitate toward collecting interesting ideas without understanding the broader context of what they mean. Calling the multitude of ideas spotted the same thing as a trend is like calling eggs, flour, and sugar sitting on a shelf the same thing as a cake. You can see ingredients, but true trends must be curated to have meaning just as a cake must be baked.

The trend-spotter myth drives many people to equate the process of identifying trends with finding a needle in a haystack. The needle-in-a-haystack cliché is so pervasive that it inspired the name for my process of curating trends: The Haystack Method.

THE HAYSTACK METHOD

The Haystack Method is a process for curating trends that starts with gathering stories and ideas and sorting them into groups that make sense (the hay), then analyzing each of the groups to see whether they reveal an underlying trend (the needle). There are five steps to the Haystack Method:

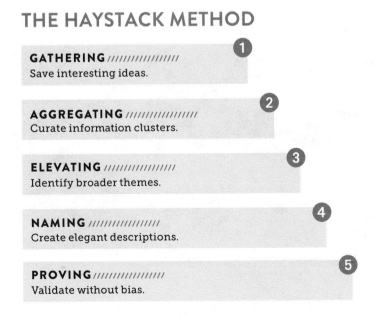

THE HAYSTACK METHOD

GATHERING ////////////
Save interesting ideas.
1

AGGREGATING ////////////
Curate information clusters.
2

ELEVATING ////////////
Identify broader themes.
3

NAMING ////////////
Create elegant descriptions.
4

PROVING ////////////
Validate without bias.
5

Gathering

Gathering is the disciplined act of collecting stories and ideas while taking notes of why they are interesting.

The best way to get value from the daily deluge of media is to form a habit of saving the most interesting stories to examine later.

How you save these stories — in a notebook, a folder on your desk, or a mobile app — is not the most important thing. The key is to give yourself a reminder of what you found interesting about the story when you saved it. This will make your notes more useful when you return to them later.

Haystack Method Step 1: Sources and methods used for Gathering

When writing reminders, keep these principles in mind:

1. **FOCUS ON INSIGHTS.** Taking notes by highlighting passages in a book doesn't work if you highlight every sentence. Don't try to summarize everything about the article or idea; instead focus on what made the idea memorable or any insights you had at the moment you saved it.

2. **ADD LABELS.** Use "note boxes" to make your notes easily skimmable. Write a few key words in a box next to your notes as a reminder why you chose the article or idea. For example, you might write BIG IDEA or BOOK TO READ in the box. Note boxes allow you to skim quickly at any time and isolate the things you want to explore further.

3. **IDENTIFY INTERSECTIONS AND APPLICATIONS.** Think about how you will apply the ideas in the articles or other pieces of content as you save them. If you don't know right away, that's okay. But if you do have an idea, make sure to capture it so you don't forget it.

DOWNLOAD A GUIDE TO NON-OBVIOUS NOTE TAKING:
www.nonobvious.com/megatrends/resources

EXAMPLE: Saving the Unusual

A few years ago I read a story about how the tomato once was known as the "poison apple" and widely feared in Europe in the 1800s. It turned out that the acidity from the tomato would interact with the lead in tableware of the time and cause fatal lead poisoning among aristocrats. Though it was certainly not a modern story, I sensed that it might relate to something more modern and saved it. A few months later, as I was writing a chapter on my 2018 trend named *Enlightened Consumption*, the tomato tidbit served as the perfect opening story.

THREE TIPS FOR GATHERING IDEAS

 START A FOLDER.
I keep a folder on my desk to store ideas written by hand, articles pulled out of magazines and newspapers, printouts from the Internet, brochures from conferences, and print ads with intrigue. The physical folder helps me to visualize the ideas and (as you'll notice from the photographs) serves as a fundamental element of how I curate ideas.

 SET A TIMELINE.
I start the clock for my annual *Non-Obvious Trend Report* every January, curate my insights throughout the year, and publish a new report every December. Thanks to the annual cycle of my efforts, I have clear starting and ending points for each new collection of ideas I curate. You don't need to follow a rigid timetable, but you still may want to set a specific schedule to review and reflect on what you have gathered so your efforts are not wasted.

 SEEK CONCEPTS, NOT CONCLUSIONS.
When identifying stories and ideas to save, don't get hung up on quantifying their value or understanding the insights behind them. Often the best thing you can do is to gather and save your idea or article, then move on to your next task. Perspective often comes from the passage of time and the patience to allow patterns to emerge on their own.

Aggregating

Aggregating is the process of grouping ideas together to uncover bigger themes.

Once you've gathered ideas, you'll need to identify how they connect to one another. Here are some questions that will help you to find the similarities among ideas:

- What broad group or demographic do these stories describe?

- What is the underlying human need or behavior revealed in these stories?

- What makes these stories interesting? What are they an example of?

Haystack Method Step 2: Aggregating articles into possible themes or topics

- How is the phenomenon the stories describe affecting multiple industries?

- What qualities or elements make these stories interesting?

During this stage, you need to resist grouping ideas by industry or topic. Instead, aggregate ideas and articles based on human motivations or broader themes. The goal is to organize small clusters of ideas and stories into meaningful groupings that you can explore and dissect later.

EXAMPLE: Finding Intersections In Ideas

Last year I gathered individual stories about several companies hiring autistic employees, Starbucks opening some coffee shops staffed entirely by deaf employees, fashion magazines hiring more models with vitiligo (a skin depigmentation condition), and marketers using stock imagery that featured more ethnically diverse models. Although the stories were related to different industries and audiences, I aggregated them all under a broad theme: "Diversity, Disability, and Inclusion." The story of fashion models with vitiligo was incorporated into a chapter about the trend of *Innovation Envy* in my 2019 report, while the story of deaf baristas was part of a trend that year called *Enterprise Empathy*. And several of these stories make a reappearance in Chapter 8 of this book as part of the *Human Mode* megatrend.

WATCH A TIME LAPSE VIDEO OF THE HAYSTACK METHOD:
www.nonobvious.com/megatrends/resources

THREE TIPS FOR AGGREGATING IDEAS

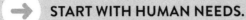

START WITH HUMAN NEEDS.
Sometimes focusing on the underlying human emotion in a story or idea can help you see why it matters and how it connects with others. For example, the basic human need for belonging fuels many activities that people engage in online, from sharing their images on social media to joining online communities.

RECOGNIZE THE OBVIOUS.
Along the path to uncovering non-obvious insights, there's value in recognizing and celebrating the obvious. For example, you can use an obvious common denominator among articles and stories to group them — say, all the stories and ideas about new wearable technology. Later you can identify the non-obvious insights hidden among them.

SAVE UNUSUAL IDEAS.
When you train yourself to be more observant, you might find that you start to develop an intuition for stories that somehow feel significant — even though you can't articulate why yet. Embrace that intuition, and always save the story. Its significance often will reveal itself later.

Elevating

Elevating involves identifying the underlying themes that align a group of ideas to describe a single, bigger concept.

Once you make it through the first two steps of this process, you may confront the same problem that I do every year: There are too many possible themes. That's normal if you are reviewing enough stories, but it's a sign that you have more work to do. This third step will help.

The goal of Elevating is to connect smaller clusters of ideas into larger ones that describe potentially bigger and more powerful trend topics. More than in any other step, this is where I find that I generate breakthrough ideas.

Haystack Method Step 3: Examples of story themes elevated to form a trend

To start elevating a group of your ideas, consider these questions:

- What interests me most about this group of ideas?

- What implications of the stories might I have missed earlier?

- What is the broader theme that these stories have in common?

- How can I link stories from multiple industries into a single idea?

This third step can be the most challenging phase of the Haystack Method. The process of combining idea clusters can lead to unintentionally grouping them into larger potential topics that are too broad and by definition, too obvious. Your aim in this step should be to identify bigger ideas that bring many stories together.

> ## EXAMPLE: Finding the Bigger Theme
>
> Several years ago I was reading about automotive manufacturers, movie theaters and software vendors all experimenting with subscription business models. At the same time, I discovered several unusual ideas for delivering products and services, from mattress vendors online to a food distribution center in the middle of Portland, Oregon. Elevating these themes to a bigger idea led me to describe the trend of *Disruptive Distribution* in 2015.

THREE TIPS FOR ELEVATING YOUR IDEAS

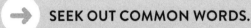

SEEK OUT COMMON WORDS.
As you review your groups of ideas and stories, look for key words that can reveal the common themes among them. When I was collecting ideas related to entrepreneurship, for example, a word kept coming up that described the growing ecosystem of on-demand services for entrepreneurs: *fast*. This word helped me bring various pieces together to identify the trend of *Instant Entrepreneurship*.

COMBINE INDUSTRY VERTICALS.
Despite my own cautions against grouping ideas by industry sector, sometimes after aggregating, I still end up with a collection of stories focused mainly on one sector. When I recognize one of these idea clusters, I look for other industry-specific clusters to combine with it. This often leads to bigger thinking and helps remove any unintentional industry bias from earlier in the process.

FOLLOW THE MONEY.
Sometimes the underlying driver of a trend has to do with who will make money from it and how. Following the money trail sometimes can lead you to make new connections.

Naming

Naming is the art of describing a collection of ideas in an accessible and memorable way.

Naming a trend is a bit like naming a child: You think of every way that the name might invite a life of ridicule, and you try to balance that with a name that feels right. At the same time, a great name should convey the trend's meaning with simplicity and be memorable.

How well you name your trend will make it either stick in people's minds and stand out — or be quickly forgotten. My second book, *Likeonomics*, took off immediately with a boost from the title, which I first defined as a trend in 2011. People promptly grasped the book's theme — that it's important to be likable because we do business with people we like — and the name was quirky enough to engage them.

Haystack Method Step 4: Sources used for names and word lists

Naming a trend can be the most creatively challenging and time-consuming part of the Haystack Method. To do it well, consider these questions:

- Is the name already in use or well understood?

- Is it relatively simple to say out loud in conversation?

- Does it make sense without too much explanation? Could you imagine it as the title of a book?

- Are the words in the name unique, not clichéd or generic?

- Does it describe a topic in an unexpected way?

Here are a few of my favorite trend names from past reports, along with a little of the backstory on the development and selection of each name.

EXAMPLES: The Art Of Naming

VIRTUAL EMPATHY (2016 + 2018). During a time when virtual reality was a hot topic, the underlying theme was that it could amplify a sense of empathy. I paired the term *virtual* with *empathy* rather than *reality* to call attention to this powerful effect.

RETROTRUST (2019). In 2019 many people were talking about nostalgia to describe the appeal of the past. But *nostalgia* seemed to bring too much emotional baggage, so I settled on *retro* because it pairs well with *trust* to summarize the simple idea behind the trend: In a world where people are becoming more skeptical of institutions and brands, they tend to place more trust in companies and brands they recognize from their past.

continued ➜

OBSESSIVE PRODUCTIVITY (2014). As the life-hacking movement generated countless stories about how to make every moment more productive, I noticed that the interest in these tools and advice bordered on obsession. To illustrate the dual nature of the trend, I combined *obsessive*, a word most people see as negative, with *productivity*, one that is usually considered positive.

While naming trends, I try lots of possibilities. I start by jotting down potential names on sticky notes, then compare the options side by side. I also test them with early readers and clients. Only after they've been thoroughly vetted do I finalize the names of the trends in that year's report.

THREE TIPS FOR NAMING YOUR IDEAS

 MASHUP WORDS.
Mashups take two words or concepts and combine them in a meaningful way. *Likeonomics* is a mashup of *likeability* and *economics*. This technique can make a trend name memorable and uniquely yours, but it can feel forced and artificial if not done artfully. There is a reason I didn't call my book *Trustonomics*. The best mashups are easy to pronounce and sound as close to a real word as possible.

 ADD ALLITERATION.
When done well, alliteration can create highly memorable and enduring names, such as Coca-Cola and Krispy Kreme. Using two words beginning with the same consonant sound is a technique I have applied to name trends such as *Muddled Masculinity (2019)* and *Disruptive Distribution (2015)*. Like mashups, alliteration can feel forced if you put two words together that aren't compatible, so use it carefully.

 GO FOR A TWIST.
By taking an obvious phrase or a commonly used term and inserting a small change, you end up with a name that surprises and stands out. One of my favorite examples is a trend I called *Unperfection (2014)*, an invented word that played off *imperfection* just enough to feel new and different.

Proving

Proving entails seeking out data, stories, and conversations to validate whether a collection of ideas can justifiably be described as a trend.

Haystack Method Step 5: Example of group collaboration to prove ideas.

The idea that a subjective curated idea such as a trend could be proven may seem like overreaching. Although I use the term *proving* to describe this step, a truer description of what you are aiming to do is *validating* your insights and conclusions.

My team and I evaluate trends using a framework of three key elements: the core idea of the trend, its impact, and its acceleration. To find out whether a trend will stand the test of time, scrutinize each of its key elements by answering the following questions:

TREND ELEMENT	USEFUL QUESTIONS TO ASK
1. IDEA. Great trend ideas are descriptions of a unique shift in culture, business, or behavior, expressed in a concise enough way to be meaningful without feeling oversimplified.	→ Is the idea unique enough to stand out? → Has anyone published research related to this trend idea?
2. IMPACT. Great trends lead people to change behavior or lead companies to adapt what they sell or how they sell it.	→ Are the media starting to uncover examples of this trend, suggesting that people and businesses are changing their behavior? → Are smart early-moving companies adopting the trend in some way?
3. ACCELERATION. Great trends typically affect business, consumer, and social behavior with speed and show signs of growing.	→ Are there enough examples of the trend across multiple industries? → Is the trend likely to continue for the foreseeable future?

During the Proving step, you're likely to find some trend ideas that do not make the cut. Leave them behind. Although it can be brutal, abandoning ideas will help you refine your insights further.

THREE TIPS FOR PROVING IDEAS

 FOCUS ON VARIETY.
One of the biggest mistakes I have seen people make when curating trends is focusing on stories or examples in a single industry. If a trend is going to describe how business is done or how consumers behave, it should be supported by examples or cases in many industries.

 WATCH YOUR BIASES.
Nothing will cloud your judgment more than starting the process of trend curation with the intent of finding trends that somehow help your industry or business. Many of the trends that are oversimplified or just plain wrong result from this flawed intention. Non-obvious trends are not self-serving.

 USE AUTHORITATIVE SOURCES.
Proving will yield better results if you have sought out authoritative sources to support your trend ideas. In practice, this means gathering stories from reputable media sources, organizations, or academic institutions.

CURATING ENGINEERED ADDICTION

Now that you have learned the five steps of the Haystack Method, let's bring the process to life by analyzing how my team and I curated a trend from a past report: *Engineered Addiction*.

STEP #1

Gathering

In April 2014, I read a story in *Rolling Stone* about a Vietnamese man named Dong Nguyen who had become an overnight celebrity thanks to his creation: a deceptively simple mobile game called Flappy Bird. The game had gone viral but he was consumed by guilt after reading reports of how thousands of people had become addicted, and were wasting time, ignoring relationships and even (in one case) losing their job. Nguyen voluntarily took his game off the Internet and it promptly disappeared. The first time I read the story, I knew it was significant — so I saved it in my yellow folder.

A few months later, I read a book called *Hooked*, which explored how Silicon Valley product designers were building habit-forming products. This seemed to describe perfectly what Nguyen had done unintentionally. I saved the book as well.

STEP #2

Aggregating

As I started aggregating ideas from my folder, I saw a pattern of stories that seemed to focus on some type of addictive behavior. The Flappy Bird story was about game design that led to addiction; the book Hooked was about creating addictive products. As I put these two ideas together, I focused on the role that interface design seemed to be playing in creating these addictive experiences. I stapled the stories together and added an index card with "Addictive Design" scribbled in black marker. It was my first description of the theme and a guess about what the trend might be.

Elevating

When I took a step back to look through my initial list of aggregated themes, several seemed related to Addictive Design. One of them was a grouping of stories I had found about the use of gamification techniques to help people of all ages learn new skills. For that group, I had an index card labeled "Gamified Learning." Another theme was a group of stories inspired by a book called *Salt Sugar Fat* that exposed how snack foods were created to offer a "bliss point" that mimics the sensations of addiction in most people. Along with the book, I had gathered several articles about popular tempting foods, a category I described as "Irresistible Food."

As I elevated my original ideas, I realized that these three unique ideas (Addictive Design, Gamified Learning, and Irresistible Food) might be elements of a single trend describing how experiences and products were created to be intentionally addictive. I grouped the elevated cluster together and called it "Ubiquitous Addiction."

Naming

After considering the ideas, I dismissed "Addictive Design" and "Gamified Learning" because they were too narrow. "Ubiquitous Addiction" didn't exactly roll off the tongue and seemed to imply that more people were getting addicted to more things, which wasn't exactly what the trend was about. The final inspiration for a better name came from an article in which Nir Eyal described himself as a "behavioral engineer." This idea of engineering addiction immediately seemed better suited to describe the trend — and *Engineered Addiction* became the trend name.

STEP #5

Proving

To test the validity of the concept and name, I enlisted the help of my team to dig further. The research soon directed us to a Harvard study about social media addiction. We then read the work of MIT anthropologist Natasha Dow Schüll, who spent more than 15 years doing field research on the addictive design of Las Vegas slot machines. Finally, we shared the rough concept of the trend in exclusive client workshops and used the early feedback to refine the idea and validate it further.

Engineered Addiction was one of the lead trends that year and quickly became one of the most talked-about trends online. It continues to drive conversations online even today.

AVOIDING FUTURE BABBLE

At this point I should share a word of caution on the dangerous potential for trend forecasting to cross over into nonsense.

We live in a world frustrated with predictions for good reason. Economists fail to predict policies that lead to global recessions. Television meteorologists predict rain that never comes. Business trend forecasters share glassy-eyed predictions that seem either glaringly obvious or naively impossible.

While I was writing the first edition of my trend report, I read journalist Dan Gardner's book *Future Babble,* about our obsession with the future. He shared the research of psychologist Philip Tetlock, who had spent more than 20 years interviewing all types of experts, including political scientists, economists, and journalists. He collected their predictions about the future — a total of 27,450. When Tetlock analyzed these predictions against verifiable data, he found that they were no more accurate than random guesses. Gardner concluded, "At least 50 percent of pundits seem wrong all the time. It's just hard to tell which 50 percent."

Tetlock described the experts who fared the worst as "hedgehogs." Overconfident and frequently arrogant, they often justified their mistaken predictions as being "almost right" and clung to one big, unchanging idea. In contrast to the hedgehogs, experts who were modest about their ability to predict the future were comfortable with uncertainty, critical of themselves, and aware that their predictions could be wrong. Tetlock described them as "foxes" and identified their defining characteristics as their ability to aggregate many sources of information, to be thoughtful about the predictions they share, and to maintain a sense of humility as they share them.

Gardner and Tetlock shine a light on a crucial point: if you are going to hone your ability to curate trends, you must embrace the notion that sometimes you will be wrong. I have accepted that reality, which led to the creation of the trend updates and ratings presented in Part 3 of this book. I share those ratings candidly (especially for trends that didn't stand the test of time) because I want to be as honest with you as I try to be with myself and my team after each year's report. Foxes, after all, are comfortable with uncertainty and know they aren't infallible. I know I'm sometimes wrong, and I guarantee that you will be, too.

WHY DOES NON-OBVIOUS THINKING MATTER?

Legendary film producer Samuel Goldwyn once said, "Only a fool would make predictions — especially about the future." He has been proven right countless times.

This book is at least partially about the future and features 10 predictions toward which time may be similarly unkind. Is doing all this work to anticipate what will happen next even worth the trouble?

Wouldn't it be better to focus on the present and try to adapt as quickly as possible to changes as they hit?

Learning to use non-obvious thinking to predict the future has a valuable side effect: It makes you more curious, observant, and understanding of the world around you. The Haystack Method can help you not only curate trends, but also find intersections between industries and avoid the trap of narrow-minded thinking. This mental shift is ultimately the greatest benefit of using the processes outlined in this chapter.

Oscar Wilde wrote that "to expect the unexpected shows a thoroughly modern intellect." *Non-Obvious* is about helping you build this type of modern intellect by noticing the things others miss, thinking differently, and curating ideas to describe the accelerating present in new and unique ways.

In the next chapter, I will show you how to put this non-obvious thinking and idea curating to work. Whether your goal is to make more money, start a business, or propel your career forward, Chapter 3 will show you how to leverage non-obvious thinking to be more successful and win the future.

03 HOW TO APPLY NON-OBVIOUS THINKING FOR FUN AND PROFIT

"Trends are profits waiting to happen."

–MARTIN RAYMOND, The Trend Forecaster's Handbook

ABOUT TEN YEARS AGO, bartenders across the world began offering an odd drink with a flavor profile like the milk left at the bottom of a bowl of Cinnamon Toast Crunch cereal. The mastermind behind the drink was Tom Maas, a former marketing executive for distiller Jim Beam.

Maas had spent years working to develop a cream liqueur based on horchata, a traditional Latin American beverage. His new liqueur, christened RumChata in honor of its inspiration, was a mixture of light rum, dairy cream, and spices such as cinnamon and vanilla. It was not an instant hit.

A unique pitch likening the drink to breakfast cereal eventually helped it break through. As the liqueur started to gain momentum, one reviewer described it as "a perfect choice for someone who wants something decadent to drink but doesn't want to get slapped across the face with alcohol."

By 2014 a combination of inventive promotions and bartender support helped RumChata earn one-fifth of the market share in the $1 billion U.S. market for cream-based liqueurs. In some regions, it started outselling the long-standing category leader, Diageo's Baileys Irish Cream. By 2019 the liqueur was one of the most popular spirit brands on social media, with more than 36 million views on its YouTube channel. Today industry experts consider the drink a crossover game changer due to its popularity as a mixer and a recipe ingredient.

RumChata is an example of the success that comes from combining the power of observation with an understanding of consumer behavior and trends. Looking back, three cultural trends might explain why RumChata was so popular:

1. A growing consumer desire for authentic products with interesting back stories.

2. The rising prevalence of food entertainment programming on television, inspiring more creativity in home cooking and spirit blending.

3. The increased interest across the United States in Latin American culture and heritage.

Of course, putting the dots together is easy looking back. Although we might be able to see these elements in the accelerating world around us, we don't always understand their immediate practical value.

Realizing those profits, though, takes more than simply uncovering and describing a trend. The most valuable trends are the ones that inspire action.

AN INTRODUCTION TO INTERSECTION THINKING

Trends might offer a signal that you should consider abandoning an existing product line or staying the course in a direction that hasn't paid off yet. Or they could suggest that you should pivot the focus of your career to learn new skills. What gives you the power to receive these signals and reach these conclusions is *intersection thinking*, a method for connecting disparate concepts and beliefs from unrelated industries to generate new ideas or products.

There are four ways to engage in intersection thinking effectively:

1. Focus on similarities.

2. Embrace serendipitous ideas.

3. Wander into the unfamiliar.

4. Be persuadable.

INTERSECTION THINKING: METHOD #1

Focus On Similarities

When former Coca-Cola executive Jeff Dunn became president of Bolthouse Farms, he walked into a billion-dollar agricultural company that had reinvented the carrot industry by creating so-called baby carrots — 2-inch-long carrot pieces that doubled carrot consumption in the United States. Unfortunately, by the time Dunn took over, sales of standard carrots and baby carrots were slumping, so Dunn turned to advertising agency Crispin Porter Bogusky (CPB[+]) for help.

The agency was struck by how much baby carrots and junk food have in common. "The truth about baby carrots," creative director Omid Farhang explained, "is they possess many of the defining characteristics of our favorite junk food. They're neon orange, they're crunchy, they're dippable, they're kind of addictive."

Using this insight, CPB[+] built the "Eat 'Em Like Junk Food" advertising campaign inspired by the marketing tactics of consumer-packaged goods companies. In campaign test markets, sales immediately shot up more than 10 percent. The spark that led to this insight came from Farhang's team's ability to translate a successful tactic from one industry (snack food) and apply it to another (agriculture). This is a perfect example not only of focusing on similarities, but also of applying the power of intersection thinking.

INTERSECTION THINKING: METHOD # 2

Embrace Serendipitous Ideas

In the mid-1980s, the idea for one of the world's most beloved brands came to life on a walk from a hotel to a convention center in Milan. Howard Schultz was at a trade show representing Starbucks, which at the time supplied high-end home brewing equipment. On the way to the convention, Schultz was struck by how many Italian espresso coffee shops he passed. These shops offered people a third place for gathering — neither their home nor their work. When he returned to Seattle, he persuaded the owners of Starbucks to create a similar retail coffee shop in the city. Years later he purchased the brand from them and took it global.

The growth of Starbucks has been remarkable, but what I find most inspiring is how it started with a serendipitous moment that Schultz might have missed. It is easy to miss serendipitous ideas because they often seem like irrelevant distractions. The truth is that sometimes they can be. The problem is that they don't come neatly labeled either way. The only way you can be open to seren-dipity is by strategically welcoming the distraction.

INTERSECTION THINKING: METHOD # 3

Wander Into The Unfamiliar

Despite an ever-expanding universe of media options to choose from, we tend to watch the same shows, visit the same websites, and read the same magazines and newspapers because we find comfort in the familiar. But what if we didn't? What if you didn't?

In Chapter 1, I noted the pleasure of reading magazines that are not necessarily targeted at you. It is one of many ways you can choose to pay attention to a world that is unfamiliar to you. Another is to wander intentionally to unusual destinations, whether they are right around the corner or a long plane ride away.

Wandering into the unfamiliar means taking a different route to the store or walking rather than driving to a nearby restaurant. It means trying a cookie made with cricket flour. It means stopping to look closely at a mural that you might have passed by numerous times.

The unfamiliar opens our mind and helps us become more innovative. Wandering helps us approach those experiences without a rigid agenda.

INTERSECTION THINKING: METHOD # 4

Be Persuadable

I have always lived in a city. Like many other city dwellers, I struggled to understand those who didn't live in one. In my mind, "country folk" seemed less cultured, less diverse and less open minded. I believed this for most of my life — until one evening when I finally realized I might be wrong.

It was late November 2015, and I had just seen the final installment of the *Hunger Games* movies. As I left the theater, I thought about other science-fiction movies and TV shows I love: *Star Wars*, *The Matrix*, and *Game of Thrones*. They share one striking detail: They feature heroic, ordinary people, often relatively uneducated, who are fighting an oppressive ruling class of pompous know-it-alls. In those stories, the country people are the good guys, and the city people are the bad guys. In an instant I suddenly realized how unfair it was to dismiss the opinions of people based solely on where they lived.

The world conspires in many ways to encourage us to burrow into the safety of our own beliefs even when we feel we aren't. Algorithms on social media serve up stories we agree with. Website cookies predict what we would like to see or might click on to buy. Polarizing politicians contend that truth demands that someone must be wrong so we can be right, and those who disagree with us should be treated as the enemy.

What if we could be brave enough to change our minds? What if we could be persuadable? What if, when we hear a compelling argument that we disagree with, we allow for the possibility that someone who sees the world in a different way might not be an idiot?

Some points of view seem so contradictory to our own that we find them hard to justify on any level. But it's possible to open ourselves to considering a different point of view. By putting ourselves in other people's shoes and imagining their back stories and reasons for behaviors, we can see the world from new angles.

THE NON-OBVIOUS WAY TO READ THIS BOOK FROM THIS POINT ON . . .

The first two chapters in this section have focused on the mindsets required to be a non-obvious thinker, and a step-by-step method to curate your ideas and develop your own trend insights. This chapter begins with the suggestion that you can use intersection thinking to find connections between ideas and use them to spot new opportunities. It is time now to focus on how to take these insights and put them into *action*. Before we do, I want to suggest an alternate method for reading the rest of this chapter. Considering these methods are most useful when you already have insights you are trying to apply. For that reason, you could continue and read these suggestions as they are presented here. Or you could now turn to Part 2, read one (or more!) of the megatrends presented there, and then return to this section to learn a model for applying them.

The beauty of a book versus any other media channel is that you can skip back and forth like this quite easily. So feel free to go to the megatrends now if you wish, or remain here and keep reading. The choice is yours.

REMAIN HERE AND JUMP TO MEGATRENDS
CONTINUE READING STARTING ON PAGE 71 →

FIVE TIPS FOR USING TREND INSIGHTS

Whether you chose to keep reading or skipped to a megatrend . . . welcome back!

Let's now explore how to put trends to work:

TREND ACTION GUIDE: FIVE TIPS FOR USING TRENDS

ENGAGE YOUR CUSTOMERS

Inspire more sales and greater customer loyalty.

SHARE YOUR STORY

Make your marketing and sales messages more relevant.

EVOLVE YOUR STRATEGY

Embrace disruption and prepare for the future.

STRENGTHEN YOUR CULTURE

Improve your employee engagement and recruiting.

DEVELOP YOUR CAREER

Build your personal brand and propel your reputation.

Engage Your Customers

Understanding and leveraging trends to improve how you engage customers starts with building a better picture of how your customers behave. One useful tool is the customer journey map—a diagram that illustrates the phases that typical customers go through when they interact with your product or service.

DOWNLOAD THE NON-OBVIOUS CUSTOMER JOURNEY MAP TEMPLATE AT *www.nonobvious.com/megatrends/resources*

Mapping this customer journey can help you understand where and when in the journey to engage in a trend to improve customers' experience and win their loyalty.

CASE STUDY: Strategic Spectacle (2019)

THE TREND

Brands, industries, and creators are increasingly resorting to big stunts to capture attention and drive engagement.

THE EXAMPLE

When Oatly, a Swedish brand that makes a dairy-milk alternative produced from the husks of oats first launched, they had a big awareness challenge. No one had ever heard of "oat milk," so the brand redesigned its packaging to feature provocative slogans such as "It's like milk but made for humans." The company placed unusually written ads in niche magazines to build the brand and hosted the world's first coffee festival without milk. Oatly's edgy approach even drew a lawsuit from the behemoth dairy industry, which the brand promptly posted online. All these stunts got attention and helped the brand explode in popularity.

Share Your Story

A powerful story can inspire support. Unfortunately, the Internet is filled with boring "about us" pages instead. These are not the same as a story. A brand story is emotional and human. It inspires people to believe in a product, brand, or message.

Trends can influence how you tell your story. What is the larger purpose behind why your brand exists? What shifts in consumer beliefs or your industry have made your existence more relevant today? These are the sorts of questions that a well-told story can help to answer.

CASE STUDY: Lovable Unperfection (2017)

THE TREND

As people seek more personal and human experiences, brands and creators focus on using personality, quirkiness, and intentional imperfections to make their products and experiences more human, authentic, and desirable.

THE EXAMPLE

The Hans Brinker Budget Hotel has been "proudly disappointing travelers for forty years, boasting levels of comfort comparable to a minimum-security prison." This is just one of the many unusual marketing messages you're likely to encounter from the Amsterdam-based Hans Brinker—the self-described "worst hotel in the world." The brand has been running advertising for more than a decade boasting about its awfulness, which has had the reverse psychological effect: People long to try it just to see how bad it really is. The brand is an extreme example of how powerful an engaging story is. It works because the backpackers traveling through Europe who typically stay at the Hans Brinker aren't seeking luxury. What they want is a great story to share with the world—and at the Hans Brinker, that's about the only thing they can count on.

Evolve Your Strategy

Tapping into trends can help you make changes to your company's strategy, whether it's evolving your business model or considering new partners to help you connect with unexpected audiences. When advising leaders on how to utilize trends for strategy, I typically encourage them to focus on five key areas:

1. **MISSION**: Why you do what you do and what you believe in.

2. **POSITIONING**: What makes your brand unique compared with that of your competitors.

3. **BUSINESS MODEL**: How you charge customers and make money.

4. **PRODUCTS AND SERVICES**: What you sell to your customers.

5. **INNOVATION**: What new products or services you may offer.

CASE STUDY: Deliberate Downgrading (2019)

THE TREND

As tech-enabled products become even more complex, consumers are downgrading to simpler, cheaper, or more functional versions.

THE EXAMPLE

Swiss entrepreneur Petter Neby may be the only CEO of a mobile phone maker who believes we don't need the Internet everywhere we go. Noticing people's increased desire to find a balanced approach to their use of technology, he created a deliberately dumb phone that has no web capability and allows only phone calls and text messages. His company's unique strategy to develop simple, elegant products that "do their job without intruding on their owner's time and attention" stands out among those of competitors determined to help us stay connected 24/7.

Strengthen Your Company's Culture

Contrary to what you might have read, you don't have to provide free food, massages, or ping-pong tables to inspire a great company culture. Workplace surveys after surveys show that what people desire most is making an authentic human connection with their co-workers feeling that their work matters, and having some autonomy over their own time. Tapping into trends can help you strengthen your company's culture in all these areas.

CASE STUDY: Experimedia (2015)

THE TREND

Brands use social experiments and real-life experiences to build trust, demonstrate human behavior in unique new ways, and build more realistic and compelling content.

THE EXAMPLE

In its early days, Zappos sold primarily shoes, and it offered two-way free shipping to help people get comfortable with buying shoes online. To reduce the return rate, the retailer built an in-house studio to record videos of employees walking in the shoes it sold. The employees who were called on to create these videos felt more valued and trusted, and the culture of the company became stronger as a result. Once these videos were added to the product page, customers got a much better sense of whether the featured shoes would work for them. Soon the return volume and costs went way down for Zappos — all thanks to a culture that enables employees to share their real-life experience with customers.

To start, assess your current culture by asking these questions:

- Do you know what the company stands for, and do you believe in its mission?

- Do you think that you have the tools and skills required to do your job every day?

- Do you feel that you are trusted to do your job independently?

- Would you recommend our business as a place for your friends to work?

- Do you generally enjoy working with your co-workers?

There is no bad time to consider how current trends might signal the need to tweak some aspects of your culture. However, it might be an urgent priority if you are about to hire many new employees, or if several employees have left within a short time. Trends can affect how you find and keep your best people.

TREND ACTION GUIDE: TIP # 5

Develop Your Career

Beyond the many ways you can apply trends in your business, you can find trends yield a significant personal benefit.

In my own life, tapping into trends has had a profound influence on where I am today. *Likeonomics*, a trend from the first edition of *Non-Obvious*, inspired me to write a book with the same title a year later. After researching the trends *Partnership Publishing* and *Precious Print* (both first published in 2013), I started my own company called Ideapress Publishing (the publisher of this book). Our *Mainstream Mindfulness* trend from 2015 led my team to develop a new workshop series for our consulting group, and the *Innovation Envy* trend from 2019 paved the way for a new *Non-Obvious Innovation* training series and executive coaching program.

CASE STUDY: Fierce Femininity (2017)

THE TREND

The rise of fiercely independent women is leading to a redefinition of femininity and traditional gender roles.

THE EXAMPLE

As women continue to rise through the ranks in business and break traditional gender expectations at work, organizations have realized that there aren't enough resources to support their aspirations. Aware of this trend, peer network groups are working to fill this void by bringing women together and giving them a place to get advice on how to deal with common challenges and to forge new business alliances.

Trends can help you anticipate the growth of an industry or offer insights into what customers are looking for, enabling you to make timely new product or service recommendations at work. They also can help you forecast what new skills you might need in the near future so you can invest time to learn them now.

Here are some other specific ways that understanding trends could boost your reputation and propel your career:

- Bolster the credibility of your ideas by backing them up with trend research.

- Share trend insights with superiors or customers.

- Connect personally with trend curators (like me!) to develop your network.

- Consider how trends might forecast a desirable industry or company to work for.

FOUR TIPS FOR RUNNING A TREND WORKSHOP

During the past decade, I've helped thousands of innovators make trends actionable within their organizations by using them to transform their business mission, rethink their customer engagement, adapt their marketing strategy, and transform their corporate culture. The ideal way to think about the potential impact of trends is like a spark that can start a fire. The trend alone is not enough, but when you use it as a catalyst for change, it can be very powerful.

The first step in doing this is often to bring the right people within an organization together for a collaborative session, which we usually describe as a *workshop*. It helps focus people's attention and offers a framework to innovate from. In case you can create a session around trends for your team or customer, here are four key elements that will help you make it a success.

TREND WORKSHOP: TIP #1:

Prepare Like A Pro

Take the time to familiarize yourself with the problems you are trying to solve: What has already been tried? What has worked or failed? What questions need to be asked in order to push the group toward real change? What are some current trends that might be applicable to the problem or issue?

TREND WORKSHOP: TIP #2:

Capture First, Critique Later

People say, "there are no bad ideas in a brainstorm." That's not true. Unfortunately, it's impossible to tell good ideas from bad ones in real time. When talking about how your business can apply or leverage a trend, encourage all participants to share ideas openly. Don't waste time and energy trying to critique them in the moment; save that for later.

TREND WORKSHOP: TIP #3:

Adopt A "Yes, And" Mindset

Improv actors successfully collaborate in a scene by going with the flow and building on one another's ideas, saying "Yes, and," then adding their own contribution. This additive approach is one of the hallmarks of effective workshops as well. If someone has an idea for how to leverage a trend, go along with it, even if you think it's unlikely to work. Then try to add to it and make it better. You never know where it might take you.

TREND WORKSHOP: TIP #4:

Always Have an Unbiased Facilitator

It's easy to assume that the person closest to the problem you hope to solve is the one most suited to lead the workshop. This is never the case. Instead, the best workshop facilitators are individuals who can lead a discussion, keep a conversation on track, and ask provocative questions without bias. They also expertly summarize the discussion, recapping any action items and ensuring that everyone who spent their precious time participating understands what they collectively achieved and what needs to happen next.

Special note for smaller teams or solo entrepreneurs: Even if you are not part of a large team, you can use a workshop to great effect.

Part of the benefit of doing a workshop, even if only two people participate, is that it gives you a moment to break from your normal routine and dedicate time to strategize for the future.

BREAKING WITH A TREND

Now that we have explored mindsets, methods and keys to putting insights into action, there is one final topic we must cover before getting to the megatrend research — the anti-trend.

As you head into reading the next section, it is possible that you will read the stories related to a particular megatrend and immediately begin thinking of an example to illustrate the exact opposite of what a particular trend or megatrend is describing. This is not a flaw in the process, it is a reality of humanity.

Trends are not mathematical theories and they don't have a single definitive answer.

They describe a behavior or shift that is accelerating and will gain in prominence or popularity, but these are not unbreakable rules of behavior. Trends involve humans and humans behave in unexpected ways.

The truth is, there will always be outliers who behave counter to trends — often intentionally. Some people and brands will see a trend and immediately lean toward trying to do the opposite just to differentiate themselves from others. In other words, they focus on the "anti-trend" on purpose.

There was a time early in my trend research when this would create a crisis of confidence for me. How could my idea possibly be a trend if I was seeing a story of someone doing the exact opposite? What I eventually came to accept is that trends aren't *laws*, they are *observations*.

Here's an analogy: If you look out your window and see most people carrying an umbrella, it's probably raining. A few people will be walking in the rain without one, getting wet either intentionally or out of necessity. But their behavior doesn't change the fact that it's raining for everyone

Curating trends can help you bring non-obvious ideas to life. It can also help you to identify what most other people or competitors will be thinking about so you can choose to strategically do the opposite.

Trends aren't meant to be followed blindly. This book is all about thinking in new and different ways. Through that lens, taking a trend and aiming to embrace its opposite certainly qualifies.

PART II
The Non-Obvious Megatrends

THE NON-OBVIOUS MEGATRENDS

AMPLIFIED IDENTITY

UNGENDERING

INSTANT KNOWLEDGE

REVIVALISM

HUMAN MODE

ATTENTION WEALTH

PURPOSEFUL PROFIT

DATA ABUNDANCE

PROTECTIVE TECH

FLUX COMMERCE

04 AMPLIFIED IDENTITY

WHAT'S THE MEGATREND?

As individualism rises globally, people are carefully cultivating how they are perceived both online and offline, chasing stardom, and making themselves vulnerable to criticism in the process.

IKUO NAKAMURA HASN'T COME OUT OF HIS ROOM for seven years. He is a *hikikomori*, a Japanese term to define a reclusive sub-genre of mostly men who haven't left their homes or interacted with others for at least six months. Some are driven to solitary existence by failing to live up to societal or parental expectations. Others retreat after being unable to cope with some big conflict.

When photographer Maika Elan published a rare photo essay and interview of the hikikomori for *National Geographic* magazine, she noted, "In Japan, where uniformity is still prized, and reputations and outward appearances are paramount, rebellion comes in muted forms, like hikikomori." Elan may have it right. The existence of the hikikomori, often chronicled in tragic terms, could represent a muted form of individuality expressed by those who can't meet the exacting demands of Japan's conforming society.

A healthier response to societal pressures is emerging in South Korea. For years, going out alone was considered something that only a social outcast (*wangda*) would do. Today a new Korean vocabulary describes individualistic activities that used to be taboo, such as *honbap* (eating alone) or *honsul* (drinking alone). A Korean colleague of mine noted that engaging in these solo activities is growing more common as they become acceptable.

The existence of the Japanese hikikomori and the rising popularity of solitary activities in South Korea are signs of how culture is shifting toward more individualistic identities.

Since 1981, researchers from the groundbreaking World Values Survey (WVS) have measured people's values and beliefs across seventy-eight countries. One of their key findings in the past two decades is a rising shift toward individualism in nearly every region of the world. This global change is contributing to an amplified sense of the importance of "self." The boldness with which we craft our identities, especially online, can empower our self-worth — or endanger it. You need only to look at what is arguably the most modern form of digital self-expression, the selfie, to see how.

THE TRUTH ABOUT SELFIES

Several years ago during a sunny spring day, my family and I were headed to one of the most popular lookouts in Arizona, called Horseshoe Bend. The site had been in the news several times in previous months for a tragic reason: It was where several tourists fell to their deaths into the canyon.

As I watched the crowd that day, it was easy to understand what made the spot so deadly. A girl was sitting on her boyfriend's shoulders, holding her camera high above her head, while the boyfriend precariously balanced on the edge of the cliff. They, like many others, were trying to take the perfect selfie with the canyon behind them. Thankfully they did manage to get their picture without fatal consequences.

Taking and posting the perfect selfie has become so important that people are literally willing to risk their lives to get the perfect one. One reason it matters so much is that selfies allow us to curate the version of ourselves that we present to distant friends and relatives whom we see rarely in real life. But how *real* is this presentation? That depends on whom you ask. Some say social media and selfies help us to express our authentic, unique identities, while others blame selfies for making an entire generation deeply narcissistic, entitled, and insecure. Award-winning journalist Will Storr explores this question in his book simply titled *Selfie*.

In the book, Storr suggests the "self-esteem myth" as the culprit behind the obsession with selfies and ourselves and thinks this has influenced how we curate our identities online. "To get along and get ahead in this new you-saturated social media arena, you had to be a better you than all the other yous that were suddenly surrounding you," he writes. "You had to be more entertaining, more original, more beautiful, with more friends, have wittier lines and more righteous opinions, and you'd best be doing it looking stylish in interesting places with your breakfast healthy, delicious, and beautifully lit."

The pressure to reach for an impossible ideal, according to Storr, might be contributing to the disturbingly high rate of depression and elevated rate of suicides — and the need for the perfect selfie in the first place. In this view, the selfie represents a dangerous reflection of our growing need for approval.

But not everyone agrees.

A CONFIDENT SELF-PORTRAIT

A more optimistic view is that selfies might actually be a conduit to *more* authenticity and confidence, rather than an insecure plea for external validation.

Girls Leadership co-founder Rachel Simmons is one such optimist. She describes the selfie as "a tiny pulse of girl pride — a shout-out to the self." In 2015, I introduced the trend of *Selfie Confidence* and agreed with her argument the selfie was deeply misunderstood. What if it was an undervalued tool for building self-esteem? When seen through this lens, the selfie could be a statement of power.

As Simmons also argued, "if you write off the endless stream of posts as image-conscious narcissism, you'll miss the chance to watch girls practice promoting themselves — a skill that boys are otherwise given more permission to develop, and which serves them later on when they negotiate for raises and promotions. A selfie suggests something in picture form — I think I look [beautiful] [happy] [funny] [sexy]. Do you? — that a girl could never get away with saying."

In telling this story about ourselves, it's easy to assume that most people would portray themselves in an exaggeratedly positive way. However, researchers are finding that people are more truthful with social media than you might expect. In many ways the public nature of social media offers more accountability because someone in your social network is likely to know when you're lying. Recent data from the Social Media Lab at Cornell University, for example, found that college students seem to be less deceptive when creating LinkedIn profiles than when writing a résumé.

Studies indicate that instead of making us self-centered liars, social media may be giving us the one thing we need to shape our identities in a digital world: power over our stories. And what's the fun of having power over our stories if we don't give ourselves the title role?

EVERYDAY STARDOM AND THE INFLUENCER REVOLUTION

Dale Carnegie, renowned author of the classic book *How to Win Friends & Influence People*, once wrote, "A person's name is to that person the sweetest, most important sound in any language." His point, made through years of observation, was that we are hard-wired to seek out moments of recognition where we feel singled out, understood, and appreciated. In a world where individualism is rising, the online world has made capturing our fifteen seconds (or less) of fame easier than ever: We can create content that portrays us as the stars of our own shows.

Consider the case of the "Bollywood Bride," a cultural phenomenon I first wrote about while introducing the trend *Everyday Stardom* — the growing expectation that the world ought to treat us like stars. Many Bollywood movies include an over-the-top musical wedding featuring flash mob–style dances and melodramatic courting rituals. These picture-perfect performances of a fantasy wedding are so popular that engaged couples across India are now are hiring film crews to recreate and capture these iconic scenes starring them, as bride and groom.

Plenty of people are finding more lasting fame as the stars of their own social media shows as well. YouTube and Instagram have made it incredibly easy for ordinary people to create content that features them talking and sharing advice about a topic they love — offering fashion and beauty product reviews, unboxing toys, playing video games live — and building an audience. Those who can build a sizable audience for their content are anointed "influencers," giving them stardom in a crowded online world and a payoff through advertising and sponsors.

As media personalities continue to emerge through social platforms and people get used to starring in their own narratives, consumers are increasingly expecting brands of all sizes to create personal experiences and make them feel like a VIP too.

This industry around identity is driving more people and brands to focus on it to attract attention and drive revenue, but there is also a downside emerging.

THE DARK SIDE OF AMPLIFIED IDENTITY

In a world where *Amplified Identity* thrives and people carefully craft how they are perceived, maintaining control over their story can be tricky. Narratives in the digital world are usually public and can therefore attract attention from unwanted cyberstalkers or lead individuals to become a target of criticism, shaming, or identity theft. Even as we look at controlling the narrative of our constructed identities, we are discovering how easily and destructively they can be dismantled.

In her book *It's Complicated: The Social Lives of Networked Teens* (2014), Microsoft principal researcher danah boyd (who spells her name without capital letters) explores how teenagers navigate this tricky online world, where attention has become a commodity. She thinks that the ease of anonymous commenting and a media culture frequently criticizing celebrities and other personalities have made responding with meanness to other people's online expressions of themselves seem normal. In this world where cyberbullying is all too common, individual identities, especially of those of young people, are under constant attack.

The challenges we face go beyond people who react with mean-ness to our posts or tweets. If we make a mistake, we can become an even bigger target. In *So You've Been Publicly Shamed*, author and documentary filmmaker Jon Ronson explores why Internet shaming has become commonplace. To understand this phenomenon, he inter-viewed people who were vilified after committing some transgression. Subjects included author Jonah Lehrer, whose plagiarism was exposed by a journalist, and Justine Sacco, a PR executive who posted a racially insensitive tweet while traveling to South Africa. Ronson concluded that by engaging in public shaming, we are "defining the boundaries of normality by tearing apart the people outside of it."

Our carefully constructed digital identities are not only vulnera-ble to criticism and shaming; but also risk being co-opted entirely. Deepfakes, consisting of superrealistic fake images and videos gen-erated by artificial intelligence, offer others the opportunity to pro-duce content that our likeness can be inserted into later.

Some technologists are building questionably ethical re-creation algorithms that could duplicate a person's voice and allow others to craft messages with it that will appear to be from a loved one after they have died. Others are taking this a step further by using past video footage to develop sophisticated holograms of public figures and even create a new functioning version of them. For example, hologram likenesses for artists such as Michael Jackson and Amy Winehouse have gone on tour, with new shows featuring real-life performers alongside these stand-ins for the dead celebrities.

The rise of questionably ethical innovations is leading to a new industry of people who are tasked with exploring these issues and crafting ground rules about who owns the digital identity of a dead person and how its integrity can be preserved.

Nevertheless, while the *Amplified Identity* trend does harbor con-siderable dangers for our identities, there is also a significant upside.

AMPLIFIED HOPE

In 2015, "America's new obsession," according to *People* magazine, was the web series called *The Keswanis: A Most Modern Family*.

The California-based Indian family included "doctor dad" Anil and "momager" Vaishali, who left her career as an optometrist to manage the exploding social media popularity of their son, "Big Nik." Nik, who has a rare form of dwarfism, built a loyal following of more than 2.5 million fans online. Rounding out the made-for-reality-TV family were his fifteen-year-old sister, Sarina, an aspiring beauty pageant star, and his six-year-old sister, Devina, a "transgender princess."

The series demonstrated an evolving willingness to embrace those who are different from us or might have been kept on the fringes of our culture in the past. I first wrote about the *Keswanis'* series in 2016 as an example of *Mainstream Multiculturalism,* a trend showing that after years of being viewed as "the other," diverse groups are finding more acceptance in mainstream culture, especially in entertainment and media.

On the surface, this trend may seem at odds with the disturbing rise of xenophobia across the world. Yet there are signs that the current climate of hate is fueled largely by a contained but loud group of anti-immigrant populists and outrage-wielding politicians who stand to profit from it. Their movements don't reflect the beliefs of most people. In fact, the evidence shows that people are becoming more accepting of others, not less. One study found that three years after Donald Trump was elected president, racial prejudice in many areas of the United States actually went down. The World Values Survey also found a widespread decrease in the number of people who responded they were uncomfortable living next to someone of a different race, which is one of the most pointed questions the survey asks to isolate racist beliefs.

It makes sense that as we develop an amplified sense of self, embrace our individuality, and share it with others, we can appreciate, accept, and even celebrate the identity of others. This is especially true for those whom our social norms cast as outsiders, an idea we also explored in 2017 with our trend *Outrageous Outsiders.* In this sense, the *Amplified Identity* megatrend, despite whatever risks it might pose to our sense of worth or the integrity of our identities, is perhaps the most hopeful of the megatrends presented in this book.

A growing worldwide shift toward individuality and the means to control our stories is driving us all to spend more time thinking about how we present ourselves. From our LinkedIn profiles to our tweets and selfies, our online identities have become the ultimate expression of who we are — or perhaps a carefully crafted self-portrait.

Like many of the other megatrends, *Amplified Identity* anticipates positive and negative changes. On the upside, this greater focus on self is having a ripple effect on people who in the past had little voice or were considered outcasts. They now can express themselves and be perceived positively, whether they are active online or not. On the downside, when our sense of self is outsized, we may become more narcissistic, more targeted for criticism, and more vulnerable to co-opting of our identities.

HOW TO USE AMPLIFIED IDENTITY

1. OVERCOME THE NARCISSISM BIAS.

The common criticism of the rise of digital identity is that it may be creating a generation of me-first monsters unable to empathize with others. If you don't fit into what some have called the selfie generation, it is tempting to condemn those who spend so much time in social media as shallow and narcissistic. Instead of judging, look past the digital tools and platforms. Remember that at the core of most social media activities is the normal desire to find one's own identity and share it with the world. That's not narcissism. It's human nature.

2. CONSIDER THE IDENTITY DIVIDE.

As our identities and relationships move online, it will become commonplace, even necessary, to share more of ourselves through digital platforms. Those who are more private and technologically averse may struggle with this new reality, and a cultural divide may arise between those who eschew online identities and those who wholeheartedly embrace the digital world. This will require a new sort of empathy and commitment to include those who are most reluctant to amplify their identities but still want and need to be part of social interactions.

3. HELP OTHERS MANAGE THEIR IDENTITY.

As our amplified sense of self continues to grow, we will turn to professionals to help us craft our identities, especially online. If you are looking for a new career, consider that a cottage industry of personal coaches, lifestyle gurus, and other self-help advisors will blossom. More unusual professions are emerging, such as "digital embalmers" who work to preserve a person's digital legacy after death. Software consultants and lawyers are stepping up to create tools or draft legislation to answer questions about online identity and privacy.

THE EVOLUTION OF AMPLIFIED IDENTITY

A review of past trends that relate to this Megatrend:

SELFIE CONFIDENCE (2015)
The ability to share a carefully crafted online
personality allows people to use social content such as
selfies (yes, selfies) to build their own confidence.

EVERYDAY STARDOM (2015)
The growth of personalization leads more consumers
to expect that their everyday interactions will be transformed
into celebrity-type experiences.

PERSONALITY MAPPING (2016)
As behavioral measurement tools map the details of
our personalities, brands start using such data to bring
like-minded people together to engage in unique experiences.

MAINSTREAM MULTICULTURALISM (2016)
After years of being minimized, multicultural citizens find
widespread acceptance through a growing integration of
diverse ideas and people in entertainment, products, and politics.

AUTHENTIC FAMESEEKERS (2017)
A new generation of creators become authentic fameseekers,
turning to social media to establish their brands, build an
audience, and become the next big thing.

OUTRAGEOUS OUTSIDERS (2017)
The rise of outsiders and their increasing willingness to
say or do the things we might describe as outrageous
to capture attention and influence.

SIDE QUIRKS (2017 + 2019)
As the global shift toward individualism continues, people
of all ages embrace what makes them unique, follow
their passion, can start a side business, and increasingly
appreciate the quirky differences in one another.

AMPLIFIED IDENTITY

05 UNGENDERING

WHAT'S THE MEGATREND?

Traditional gender divisions and labels are getting replaced with a more fluid understanding of gender identity, forcing a reevaluation of how we see employees, customers, brands and one another.

I WAS PUTTING THE FINISHING TOUCHES on the seventh edition of *Non-Obvious* in 2017 when I noticed something unusual in the signature of an email I had just received. Beneath the sender's name and title was this line: "My preferred pronouns are them/they." A few days later, I received an email from someone else with a similar signature: "My preferred pronouns are she/her." I realized immediately that this new signature convention was the latest sign of a shift in gender that I had been tracking for years before I even started the research for the first edition of the trend report back in 2011.

In 2008, as I was completing the research for my first book, *Personality Not Included*, I discovered it was far easier to find great stories online of pioneering businessmen than similar stories about women. To try to remedy the inequality, I launched something I called the Personality Project to spotlight the stories of forty successful women. The insights I gained in this work eventually led me to publish our first gender-related trend in 2013: *Powered by Women*.

Since then, our traditional understanding of gender roles has been challenged and broken down. Gender was once a simple binary choice: You were either female or male. Although our traditional understanding of gender roles has evolved since the 1970s, email signature lines like the ones I received would have seemed unfathomable even ten years ago.

But things are changing quickly. In early 2014, Facebook expanded its previously limited gender options for personal profiles to include fifty-eight new ones. Less than a year after that announcement, the social platform list grew to more than seventy options and included a free-form field where users could create their own gender label or forgo adding one altogether.

Three years later, *National Geographic* magazine devoted an entire issue to "the gender revolution," which was turned into a documentary film about gender identity, produced, and narrated by journalist Katie Couric. As she interviewed scientists, psychologists, activists, authors, and families about gender, she asked all kinds of questions. What is gender? What is intersex? How many gender classifications do we need?

The documentary didn't offer any definitive answers to the questions, but it did make clear that many people no longer consider gender to be a label determined at conception. Instead, it is increasingly accepted as a choice that we make for our current selves and maybe even evolve throughout our lifetime. Moreover, the words used to describe gender are expanding and include terms such as *nonbinary, genderless, nonconforming, gender fluid, trans, agender,* and *polygender.*

We are living in the time of *Ungendering.* As the stereotypes of feminine and masculine ideals are supplanted, the traditional labels and roles once prescribed to our identities based on gender are no longer as meaningful. This is leading to an evolved view of what role gender should play in the products we buy, the experiences we enjoy, and even the way we define ourselves.

For a growing number of organizations, this is forcing a fundamental reimagining of basic assumptions and messaging in marketing, merchandising (men's and women's sizes), and how they deliver services or even categorize their products themselves.

A FIERCE FEMININITY MOVEMENT

An increasing number of powerful female characters emerged from the film and publishing industries over the past decade. Best-selling dystopian teen book series such as *The Hunger Games* and *Divergent,* for example, feature strong leading women. *Girl Rising* and other award-winning documentaries are sparking a global conversation about the importance of educating girls. And culture-shifting television series such as *Orange Is the New Black* and *Game of Thrones* feature complex female characters going through personal transformations. The emergence of these characters reflects a shift in how women are defining their roles and femininity, a trend I first described in 2017 as *Fierce Femininity*.

One example is a graphic novel called *Priya's Shakti*. Even by superhero back-story standards, Priya's is extremely violent. Introduced at the Mumbai Comic and Film Convention in 2014, the story centers on a village girl named Priya who survived a gang rape and goes on a mission to stop violence against women. When it first appeared, the novel, which offered a bold model for a fierce heroine who could inspire a new generation of girls, was downloaded more than half a million times.

A matter of months after the book went to print, the #MeToo movement began sweeping the internet. The hashtag became a rallying cry for women who shared their stories of being sexually harassed or assaulted in the workplace. A year after it went viral, the *New York Times* determined that about two hundred powerful men had been fired after public allegations of sexual harassment were made against them. By the newspaper's count, women replaced half of those men in their jobs. As best-selling author and screenwriter Gillian Flynn pointed out in an interview, "Ultimately [women] are coming alive because they are finding rage and finding their empowerment and pushing back."

In the 1970s, for many, the ideal of femininity was a woman who "has it all"—a job and a family and a household to take care of. Later women were celebrated for being the "jugglers-in-chief" and expected to uphold impossible standards in the workplace and at home. This facade is now falling at breakneck speed, replaced by an unapologetically fierce model of femininity. Women can be and are strong and serious. They can be mothers, or they can choose "otherhood," a term author Melanie Notkin coined to describe women who by choice or "circumstantial infertility" (never meeting the right person) don't have children. Women are getting married later if at all, pursuing higher education in greater numbers than men, starting more companies, and "taking their seat at the table," as Flynn points out, instead of waiting for someone to give it to them.

Yet while this shift in women and femininity has been more than a decade in the making, a corresponding evolution of men and masculinity has only taken hold and started accelerating far more recently.

MUDDLED MASCULINITY

When I was in middle school, my favorite book series was *Sweet Valley High*, which followed the lives of Jessica and Elizabeth Wakefield, perfect blonde identical twins from the fictional town of Sweet Valley, California. Often called "teen Harlequins," these books were highly popular in the 1980s and inspired young readers to turn to books instead of TV. Young female readers, that is. As series author Francine Pascal told the *Los Angeles Times* in an interview, "The truth is, boys read until about age 12, then they go outside and don't come back in until they are about 18."

I remember loving to go outside, but every time I came back in, it would be to read another story about the romantic adventures of Jessica and Elizabeth. I also remember, with some embarrassment, how odd it was for a boy to be checking out five or six *Sweet Valley High* books at a time from the library. On more than one occasion, I'm sure the librarian assumed I was getting them for my nonexistent sister. A boy reading about love, relationships, and high school drama was out of the ordinary.

In the time since, even as our perspectives on female gender roles have shifted dramatically, how we perceive masculinity and fatherhood remains confused and one-dimensional. There is evidence that this uneasiness is leading to anxiety among men and boys about what it means to be a man today, a trend we described as *Muddled Masculinity* in the 2019 edition of our trend report.

In June 2018, the opinion-polling website FiveThirtyEight commissioned a survey of 1,615 adults who identify as men. The pollsters wanted to find out whether the recent media attention given to gender inequality and sexual harassment in the workplace after #MeToo had changed men's thinking on masculinity. The results were conflicted. Fifty-three percent of surveyed men said it was important for them that others see them as masculine. Forty-nine percent reported always trying to pay the bill when out on a date. More than half felt that in the wake of the #MeToo movement, it was a disadvantage to be male at work as men "are at a greater risk of being accused of sexual harassment." The survey results suggested that even as other parts of our culture face a reckoning over gender roles and inequality at work, many men continue to feel the same pressures of society to adhere to a traditional but outdated ideal of what it means to be a man.

In a powerful piece for the *Atlantic*, writer Sarah Rich hypothesizes that approaching gender equality by focusing exclusively on empowering girls has unintentionally reinforced the idea that girls who embrace more traditionally masculine behaviors, such as being assertive and courageous, will be more successful, while boys who embrace more traditionally feminine behaviors, such as being kind and cooperative, will not. "When school officials and parents send a message to children that 'boyish' girls are badass, but 'girlish' boys are embarrassing, they are telling kids that society values and rewards masculinity, but not femininity," Rich concludes. "When boys get this message, it reinforces the confusing belief that there is only one way to be a boy (and, by extension, only one way to act like a man). And that way doesn't involve engaging in any activity that is seen as being 'for girls.'"

What does it mean? Sadly, even today, a young boy checking out *Sweet Valley High* books at the library probably would raise a few eyebrows.

MALE CONFUSION

The confusion that men feel about what it means to be masculine today is in no small part fueled by media and cultural stereotypes. While women are getting more gender-empowered messages from advertisers ("You can do anything!"), men often see themselves portrayed as the same incompetent, beer-chugging, lovable doofuses interested only in fun. Although there's widespread dissatisfaction with these stereotypes, the ads endure. A recent survey from MDG Advertising found that 85 percent of fathers said they knew more than advertisers give them credit for, and 74 percent of millennial fathers felt that advertisers and marketers were "out of touch with modern family dynamics."

Some advertisers are starting to take notice. Barbie dolls are now marketed to girls *and* boys. Tide detergent featured well-known NFL quarterback Drew Brees doing laundry, cleverly rebranding him as the "equipment manager of the household." However, these occasionally progressive images in the media have not moved the needle enough. The workplace still hasn't caught up with modern family dynamics. After several decades of debating and dismissing the stereotype that mothers should stay home and take care of the kids, our culture has yet to grapple seriously with the "stuck-at-work-dad" stereotype of the father who should have the 9-to-5 (or longer) job.

Even today, fathers in dual-income households are expected to be the primary family provider, according to a Pew report. Mothers are disproportionally expected to balance their job with their kids' doctors' appointments and grocery shopping. These expectations prevail in many companies, where it is often not culturally acceptable for men to leave early to attend a school function even though the official company policies might allow it.

"Boasting about your latest diaper victory isn't yet a normal part of guy talk," writes Brittany Levine Beckman in *Mashable*. "Even taking paternity leave can still be perceived as weak." The result is that men are expected, and willing, to be supportively, equal partners and emotionally available fathers, but they struggle to balance those demands with workplaces that don't accommodate them and instead make it harder to prioritize their family above work.

WHY TESTOSTERONE MAY BE OVERRATED

For years, the idea that there is an intrinsic difference between men and women was fodder for everything from stand-up comedy routines to marriage counseling approaches. Men and women, to sum up the argument, are born different, or as John Gray titled his popular book from 1992: *Men Are from Mars, Women Are from Venus*. But what if they aren't?

Psychologist and professor Cordelia Fine, as well as other prominent researchers, have branded this idea an unacceptable form of neurosexism. In her books *Delusions of Gender* (2010) and *Testosterone Rex: Myths of Sex, Science, and Society* (2017), she challenges the assumption that men's and women's brains are inherently different. More specifically, she disputes the common theory that testosterone, which is present more abundantly in male brains than female ones, makes men better suited for some tasks and women better suited to others. She believes this theory is the basis of almost every gender stereotype. Men are more logical thinkers; women are more nurturing. Men are more decisive; women are better collaborators.

Fine's ideas are so unconventional that some read them as a personal attack on gender and perhaps their own identity. Just six months after *Testosterone Rex* was published, nearly half of the reviews on Amazon gave it a single star—an unusually high number that most likely reflects the polarized political response to her research rather than its inherent value. Fine's work, however, is only one example of the transformation taking place today in how we understand, relate to, and discuss gender issues beyond male and female.

GENDER X

Though the concept of a nonbinary gender identity still might seem like a fringe idea, there are signs that this often-misunderstood label is gaining mainstream acceptance across the world. There is a growing understanding that a person's gender can differ from that person's sex.

A newborn's sex is assigned at birth based on the baby's genitalia. Gender, however, is to many a question of identity; it's how you carry yourself and interact socially with the world. For a growing number of people, gender is never described in singular terms but rather along a spectrum depending on how they present themselves to the world. Jonathan Van Ness, one of the stars of the Netflix show *Queer Eye*, perhaps summed up this perspective on gender best in an interview for *Out* magazine: "I'm gender nonconforming. Like, some days I feel like a man, but then other days I feel like a woman."

At the time of this writing, more than ten U.S. states have passed legislation allowing individuals to select a gender-neutral choice of X (this is the letter used instead of M or F) on their driver's license and ID cards. Over the past decade, about a dozen countries, including Australia, Germany, Canada, and India, also have allowed for a third gender option on passports.

As nations around the world become more accepting of nonbinary gender status, companies and brands are responding by reshaping the products and experiences they sell to fit into this new world of *Ungendering*.

UNGENDERED CONSUMPTION

In 2016, CoverGirl announced its first male spokesmodel, seventeen-year-old James Charles, whose photo shoots quickly went viral. Just two years later, Chanel released Boy de Chanel, its first makeup line targeted at men. Clinique, Tom Ford, Glossier, and other brands followed suit, and it's likely the rest of the industry will too. According to Allied Market Research, the value of the men's personal care market is expected to reach $166 billion by 2022 with an annual growth rate of over 5 percent.

Products made for children, such as clothes, toys, and home goods are all moving away from pointlessly gendering their products. Citing a widespread backlash against pink and blue branding, many toymakers are creating more inclusive packaging and avoiding attaching a gender to products, particularly those targeted at preschool-age children.

The transition to gender-neutral toys hasn't been entirely smooth, however, as LEGO learned in 2012 when it launched its controversial line LEGO Friends, designed specifically for girls. The criticism was immediate. Parents and journalists alike demanded to know why girls needed special pink LEGOs. Rather than issuing a panicked recall, LEGO started communicating just how much research had gone into developing a special line for girls (four years' worth of interviews with 4,500 girls and moms globally) and explaining why it was a good idea.

Customers agreed. The LEGO Friends line was a smash hit, driving record profits for the company and successfully attracting more girls to buy and play with the plastic blocks and figures, a challenge for the brand since it was founded more than eighty years ago.

That a product line designed to look so "traditionally girlie" was a hit suggests that untangling gender from products is not easy or straightforward. After all, kids receive social cues about what is acceptable for girls and for boys from infancy. Biases take time, often generations, to change.

Yet there are signs that this process is accelerating. According to a recent survey from the insights group at advertising giant JWT, "82 percent of Gen Zers [people born between 1995 and 2015] think that 'gender doesn't define a person as much as it used to.'" This generation of young people seems unwilling to accept the limits traditional gender roles once placed on their identities, not to mention what they choose to enjoy or whom they choose to love.

The future, in other words, belongs to those for whom traditional genders are no longer meaningful — and those who think like them.

UNGENDERING AT A GLANCE

Perhaps no other trend confronts something that feels as fundamental to our culture as gender identity or has as much potential to change how we live and relate to one another. When gender is no longer the first question or the framing lens from which we live our lives, it will create confusion as well as opportunities for those who are willing to reinvent themselves, what they make, and how they interact with their teams, their customers, and those around them accordingly.

In some cases, this will lead to controversy as slower-moving leaders and brands will miss opportunities or make missteps that are quickly outed by sensitive consumers. More positively, there will be plenty of new opportunities to open the market for previously gendered products and experiences to more diverse audiences, foster an even more inclusive workplace, and benefit from the diverse perspectives of those who see gender as a spectrum rather than a binary choice.

1. REMOVE UNNECESSARY GENDERING.

In a world where people are rediscovering what role gender identity plays in the experiences they love, the products and services that will succeed are those that are inclusive and empathetic. Look closely at your current products and services, especially how they are packaged and marketed, and consider how you can remove unnecessary gendering and make them more inclusive and expansive.

 2. ENCOURAGE NONTOXIC MASCULINITY.

When men or boys express a passion or curiosity for exploring traditionally feminine things, avoid making quick judgments and instead encourage them. To reinforce these experiences, consider using nonconforming images and messaging when portraying men and their relationships to women to encourage nontoxic views of masculinity and ensure the men, and particularly boys, feel it is acceptable to love what they love, share their emotions more openly, and treat all people with respect regardless of gender identity.

 3. HAVE MORE GENDER EMPATHY.

Shifting one's thinking to consider gender as being on a spectrum rather than binary is not easy. Yet leaders, teachers, and politicians who do will become far more effective because they will earn the respect and loyalty of those who previously were considered outcasts and finally feel understood.

THE EVOLUTION OF UNGENDERING

A review of past trends that relate to this Megatrend:

POWERED BY WOMEN (2013)

Business leaders, pop culture, and groundbreaking research intersect to prove that our ideal future will be led by strong and innovative women working on the front lines.

ANTI-STEREOTYPING (2014 + 2016)

Across media and entertainment, gender roles start to reverse, assumptions about alternative lifestyles are challenged, diversity increases, and perceptions of how people are defined continue to evolve.

FIERCE FEMININITY (2017)

The fierce, independent woman has emerged in recent years, redefining the concept of femininity and reimagining gender roles.

UNGENDERED (2018)

Shifting definitions of traditional gender roles are leading some to reject the notion of gender completely, while others aim to mask gender from products, experiences, and even their own identities.

MUDDLED MASCULINITY (2019)

The rising empowerment of women and the reevaluation of gender are causing widespread confusion and angst about what it means to be a man today.

UNGENDERING

06 INSTANT KNOWLEDGE

WHAT'S THE MEGATREND?

As we become accustomed to consuming bite-sized knowledge on demand, we benefit from learning everything more quickly but risk forgetting the value of mastery and wisdom.

WHEN I WAS IN COLLEGE there were two types of classes: lectures and discussions. In lectures, a room full of students listen to an expert presenting a topic or subject; and in a discussion class, professors or teaching assistants lead small groups of students in a meaningful exchange about the assignment of the week. As an English major, I attended more discussion-style classes than lectures.

During my third year at Emory University in Atlanta, I remember taking a class on Irish poetry in a library that housed the collected archives of Nobel Prize–winning poet Seamus Heaney. That same semester I took a science class right next to the world-renowned Yerkes National Primate Research Center.

Back then, the only way to access that type of knowledge about either subject was to enroll in a course and learn from professors during a long semester.

Today I can go online and watch dozens of interviews with Heaney, along with a one-hour documentary about his life. I can access a lecture on the evolution of "brain asymmetries in primates" on YouTube, or I can sign up for an online class about them. But watching interviews or lectures online is not the equivalent of engaging in a lively classroom debate among peers or interacting in person with a renowned mind. Nevertheless, it's a substitute of sorts, and for better or worse, the world seems increasingly willing to make this compromise.

Today experts are no longer found only in the ivory tower of academia, putting its value in question. Instead, they may be celebrities or amateur experts who are finding new ways to share their knowledge. Yet knowledge — a term that superficially describes what you *know* — is different from wisdom. The benefits of this *Instant Knowledge*, as this megatrend is called, also may be leading to a crisis of expertise itself. What does expertise mean in a world where we can learn a little bit about anything from anyone without the need to seek mastery? And what happens to the institutions that have long promised to offer a gateway to mastery when it no longer seems as important to attain it?

A HIGHER EDUCATION CRISIS

By some estimates, the amount of student-loan debt in the United States has surpassed $1 trillion. Some sensational, though not entirely inaccurate, reports predict that the average cost for a single year at a private university for a child born in 2020 could be as high as $500,000. Yet students are not necessarily getting what they are paying for even as the costs of higher education soar. More universities are increasing spending on athletics instead of academics. Critics of academia are raising concerns about the true effectiveness and fundamental value of the system. One of them is Kevin Carey, the author of *The End of College.* "Evidence of student learning is almost totally absent from traditional college degrees," he writes. "Colleges don't systematically concern themselves with the quality of the teaching and learning they provide in exchange for large amounts of money."

Also raising questions about the value of higher education are the highly visible examples of wildly successful entrepreneurs who wear their lack of a college degree like a badge of honor. The college-dropout-turned-Silicon-Valley-billionaire trope has undermined the unshakable belief that one must go to college to succeed and replaced it with the perception that there are many alternate paths to success. Trade and vocational schools that offer certifications and focus on real-world preparatory courses are gaining popularity with the newest generation of students. Advances in e-learning technology are making learning of all sorts available on demand, accessible outside the confines of universities, and divorced from earning a university degree — a trend we called *Degree-Free Learning* in 2013.

LEARNING FOR SELF-STARTERS

In response to these shifts in higher education, nontraditional organizations of many types are emerging to satisfy people's desire to learn and prepare for the demands of today's careers. Tech School 42, an experimental computer programming school based in Paris, offers a radically different alternative to universities. Founded in 2013 by French billionaire Xavier Niel, who taught himself how to code and thinks that anyone can do the same, the school is completely free and has no teachers and no classrooms. Students study and learn at their own pace. When they encounter problems, they are encouraged to ask one another or just figure it out themselves.

The school places a high value on ambition and contends that those who are self-motivated and driven to work independently can succeed. This self-starter ethos is catching on. Some innovative schools are focusing on the "60-year curriculum," which involves many institutions of higher education providing continuing education based on certificates and short courses focused on tangible job skills or cutting-edge topics.

Just two decades ago, the Generation X mindset of the Nineties often was criticized as a lazy "slacker culture." Today people have outgrown this mindset. They are curious, ambitious, and willing to learn although strapped for time. They think they're smart and believe they can absorb and understand any topic quickly if it's taught by reputable experts in an accessible way.

I first described this type of person as the "Time-Starved Doer," a segment my team and I aimed to engage with the *Non-Obvious Guide* book series that we launched in 2019. This mindset led to our tagline for the series: "Like having coffee with an expert." It is meant to represent a new truth about how people want to learn: by accessing experts and expertise directly. Perhaps the biggest impact of this shift is not necessarily how we learn, but rather how *quickly* we expect most learning to happen.

LIGHT-SPEED LEARNING

Andy Mooney, CEO of Fender, which has made some of the world's finest guitars for more than seventy years, estimates that about 90 percent of students who pick up the guitar quit within the first year. This is bad not only for music but also for Fender's bottom line. What would it take to get people to stick with it? After extensive interviews with teachers and students asking this question, Mooney and his team gained a critical insight: When students feel that they are not progressing quickly enough, they are more likely to quit. The secret to encourage aspiring guitarists to persist is to help them learn to play in smaller steps so they feel they are getting better more quickly. So Mooney's team developed Fender Play, an online platform that offers video instruction on demand. It was a hit. Fender Play served as an example of a trend I described in 2018 as *Light-Speed Learning* — the idea that the speed of acquiring a new skill is more important than ever.

Plenty of evidence indicates that this trend is not slowing down. One example is the popular Tasty cooking videos, which use a time-lapse format to offer cooking techniques and recipes. In 2017 the channel reported half a *billion* views on Facebook every month. Another service, Flocabulary, provides access to a library of more than a thousand videos of original hip-hop songs about school subjects such as history, math, science, and grammar. Its success relies on a simple truth: Songs are easier to memorize than flash cards.

Today we are turning to online videos for help with doing math homework, balancing a checkbook, or becoming a better basketball player. These packaged nuggets of instant knowledge not only provide the fastest way to learn about a topic, but also give on-demand access to experts who were previously too busy or otherwise impossible to access . . . even celebrities.

GOING STRAIGHT TO THE SOURCE

Online content often is derided because it allows anyone to share his or her thoughts and creations, good or bad, with the world. This same ubiquity, though, is starting to offer a fascinating side benefit: access to learn from renowned experts. Want to learn comedy from Steve Martin? Photography from Annie Leibovitz? Chess with Garry Kasparov? They all have online classes where they share their expertise with anyone for a relatively low fee.

Technology also is employed to teach practical skills in realistic simulations. Virtual reality and other immersive digital tools are helping the plumbing and heating industry improve its certification training programs. The medical industry is using virtual tools to help students learn anatomy, develop better communication skills with patients, and even learn surgical techniques from more experienced surgeons. At more than a dozen facilities across the United States and Europe, delivery giant UPS is using virtual reality training modules to prepare its drivers for potential hazards on the road.

As these immersive digital tools change how and where we learn, the idea of expertise itself is becoming more inclusive, less classroom oriented, and more widely available. This is a trend I first wrote about in 2014 as *Distributed Expertise*.

Yet these instant lessons do introduce a new problem. We don't always process knowledge that we acquire quickly the same way as when we learn something more slowly or thoughtfully. While we know a little about a lot, people who know a lot about a little risk becoming a dying breed. Entire segments of human knowledge — the kind that takes a long time to acquire — are disappearing.

THE DEATH OF LANGUAGE AND TRADITIONAL SKILLS

Every two weeks, a language dies. According to the *UNESCO Atlas of the World's Languages in Danger*, more than 230 languages have gone extinct over the past seventy years. Another 2,500—nearly half the world's remaining languages—are endangered at some level. Many digital initiatives are under way to record some of these languages before their last living speaker dies. But even if these efforts succeed, many of the languages preserved may live on only in a database.

Rare languages have met with inevitable death for centuries. As our world becomes more connected, the need to speak a diversity of languages has been slowly decreasing. Today, knowing a language spoken by only a few people is a liability because it limits a person's prospects for succeeding in the global economy.

However, as a language dies, what is often lost alongside it is deep wisdom. The way the language describes the human condition, reveals mysteries of our past and contains possibilities in a way that can't be translated. As deep wisdom and mastery of languages die, so might our ability to reveal and understand more about our past and, often, wisdom about how we and our planet can survive in the future.

Almost any traditional skill our forebears once mastered, from relying on celestial navigation to hunting and gathering food, may suffer a similar fate. As people no longer need to exercise these skills to survive, they lose their ability to do them at all. Although this process has been gradual, today as a species we are no longer adept at the things humans were once uniquely skilled at, from tracking to throwing. Our knowledge of edible and medicinal foods has similarly been shrinking.

One disturbing study even suggested millennials may contend with a widespread loss of grip strength due to the growing amount of time spent with technology instead of doing more physical activities. This reliance on technology also may be changing the way our brains work, a point author Nicholas Carr noted in his 2010 book *The Shallows*. Witnessing a shift in his own thinking, he wrote,

"Once I was a scuba diver in the sea of words. Now I zip along the surface like a guy on a Jet Ski."

SHORTCUT CULTURE

When we don't earn our knowledge to do and make things, we may fail to appreciate its significance. As we steadily find shortcuts to improve our jobs and life, we undervalue the importance of developing mastery. Today's technologies are increasing that danger as they create ways to avoid the one vital requisite to learning any skill or achieving any mastery: practice.

For the past decade, a small team of scientists at Georgia Tech's GVU Center has studied *passive haptic learning,* "the acquisition of sensorimotor skills without active attention to learning." They've developed a glove, for example, that delivers electrical pulses to subconsciously create a "muscle memory" and teach people tactile tasks, such as how to read Braille or play the piano, without active attention. In early tests, the method was shown to help people learn tasks that ordinarily would take weeks or months of practice in a matter of hours.

Neuralink, an Elon Musk–funded company in San Francisco, is working to develop implantable brain-computer interfaces that could improve memory and allow the human mind to link directly with a computer. Scientists describe our brain's ability to adapt to new stimuli and form new neural pathways as *neuroplasticity*. For example, tests have found significantly greater gray matter density (associated with higher cognitive abilities) in bilingual people than among people who speak a single language. What if we could turn to technology to help increase anyone's gray matter density, without any effort on their part at all?

For years, this type of effortless learning has been the realm of science fiction. Keanu Reeves's character Neo from *The Matrix* film series, for example, just plugs in to download skills such as martial arts directly into his brain. In the future this type of learning may become common. But in the meantime we are moving towards this vision in smaller, more realistic ways every day as the Instant Knowledge megatrend grows.

We can learn almost anything more quickly and easily, sometimes from authoritative amateurs and sometimes from renowned experts. As this information becomes more easily accessible, and the costs of higher education spiral uncontrollably, the perceived value of on-demand learning will continue to grow. Yet this megatrend comes with a concerning downside.

Will we become a society where quick sound bites and surface knowledge replace depth and wisdom? Worse yet, if we are creating a generation fueled by the expectation of quick learning and lacking the patience or capacity for deeper learning, can we trust the longevity of the things they build or the safety of the services they provide? These are the sorts of questions we will struggle with in the future. They probably will lead those who provide education, as well as anyone with anything to teach, to constantly reinvent how they share their knowledge with the world.

1. SPEED UP YOUR CONTENT.

Ten percent of listeners of audiobooks increase the speed of the narration. A similar percentage of students from Khan Academy watch videos at a faster pace. One recent study found that speeding up content has no negative impact on comprehension. Given the little amount of time and the overload of content we receive daily, speeding up how we consume content has become a smart, even necessary, way to learn. While it may not lead toward wisdom and may even hinder the ability to see bigger themes (or trends — as I share in Part I), knowledge can indeed be attained faster.

2. OFFER ON-DEMAND LEARNING.

As most consumers today know, the best way to get directions for fixing an electronic device or a leaky faucet isn't by reading the manufacturer's instructions. It's by watching videos on YouTube that offer simple, straightforward directions for how to do it. Companies that collaborate with experts to offer these on-demand resources for their products have an opportunity to create lasting bonds with their customers by helping them get smarter.

3. BECOME A DEEP EXPERT.

In a world where people know a little about a lot, those with decades of experience in a trade, craft, or skill will be more valued for their knowledge. If you want to succeed in coming years when *Instant Knowledge* is likely to accelerate, one way to do it is to balance fast self-learning with deeper intentional mastery of a topic, subject, or skill.

THE EVOLUTION OF INSTANT KNOWLEDGE

A review of past trends that relate to this Megatrend:

DEGREE-FREE LEARNING (2013)
The quality of e-learning content explodes as more students consider alternatives to traditional college educations.

↓

METHOD CONSULTING (2013)
Successful entrepreneurs and companies create on-the-side consulting models to help others duplicate their success.

↓

DISTRIBUTED EXPERTISE (2014)
As online platforms offer access to learn directly from experts, expertise itself becomes more inclusive, less academic, and widely available on demand.

↓

LIGHT-SPEED LEARNING (2018)
The road to mastery on any topic accelerates with the help of bite-sized learning modules that make education more efficient, engaging, useful, and fun.

INSTANT KNOWLEDGE

07 REVIVALISM

WHAT'S THE MEGATREND?

Overwhelmed by technology and a sense that life is now too complex and shallow, people seek out simpler experiences that offer a sense of nostalgia and remind them of a more trustworthy time.

THERE IS A MOMENT during the fourth season of the popular comedy series *The Office* when bumbling but lovable manager Michael Scott decides to create a TV ad for his company, Dunder Mifflin. The ineffectually hilarious tagline he lands upon for the paper company, "limitless paper for a paperless world," is at once ironic, silly, and profound.

There are signs that a paperless world may indeed be inevitable.

Long-running magazines such as *Newsweek* and *Teen Vogue* have announced they are shifting to digital-only publications. According to PwC's Global Entertainment & Media Outlook 2018-2022, "sales of physical video games, recorded music, and home video are expected to decline each year, in some instances by double-digit percentages." Yet one form of media has proven remarkably resistant to this shift: printed books.

The same PwC report also notes that sales of physical books are expected to grow modestly during the next several years. I have seen this reality myself through the preferences of my children. Whenever I ask my kids whether they want to read a book as an ebook or a "real book," they always pick the latter.

In other product categories, there is a generational gap between the preferences of the young and the old. Studies show that younger people, for instance, prefer texting while older people prefer talking on the phone. But the fondness for physical books seems to cut across ages and demographics. Industry insiders have offered a few logical explanations for this. People like to take notes in the margins of books. Reading physical books causes less eye strain than reading on a screen. And many people do enjoy turning pages by hand and savoring the distinctive smell of a book.

While these arguments make intuitive sense, it's possible there is a deeper explanation.

Since 2013, I have been tracking the growth in popularity of physical notebooks, online art auctions, board games, vinyl records, and other products that combine tactile elements with a touch of nostalgia. We cataloged these shifts through two trends, *Precious Print* (2013) and *Touchworthy* (2018). Both explore how we increasingly value things that we can hold in our hands and experience in a tactile way. These items feel more significant precisely because we spend so much of our lives in the digital realm. The photos we print and display, for example, hold an added significance apart from the thousands we take and then archive in our phones or on the cloud, never to be seen again.

Today we see a broader shift happening. As we become overwhelmed by a general sense that life has become too complex, we are finding solace in items, products, and experiences that are more nostalgic, such as a book or a board game, and reminiscent of a simpler time in our lives.

This shift is at the heart of the megatrend *Revivalism*, which explains everything from our growing desire for less tech-enabled products, to the resurgent appeal of artisan crafts and iconic retro brands, to our desire to preserve our history and the simpler times and the "good old days" it represents.

SIMPLER TECH FROM A SIMPLER TIME

While technology and design often promise to make things better, faster, and smarter, sometimes the latest version of a product is not as functional, durable, safe, economical, or simple to use as earlier versions were. Automated self-driving cars promise safety and convenience, but potentially can be hacked. Toys, clothing, dishware, and countless other retail products seem to be manufactured more cheaply than in the past and are therefore far less durable.

There is even a term in technology circles, *bricking*, that describes a piece of technology being damaged or rendered unusable by an inability to have its software updated. Today anything from a cell phone to a smart car can be turned into an expensive but useless brick.

Sometimes the downside of this overreliance on technology can be deadly, as it was in 2019 with the tragic crashes of two Boeing 737 Max planes. The accidents were apparently caused by a software malfunction of a new feature that took control of the aircraft away from pilots and erroneously pointed the nose of the plane down even as crew members desperately and unsuccessfully tried to get control back from the computer.

Thankfully, the consequences of newer and smarter technology, even if it malfunctions, aren't typically this dire. However, tragedies such as the Boeing 737 crashes are fueling a growing belief that so-called "upgraded" technology may not always be better. Instead, sometimes it is the older, slower, and dumber option that becomes more desirable.

When I first wrote about this shift in 2016, we described it as a trend called *Strategic Downgrading*. Three years later the trend evolved slightly to *Deliberate Downgrading*. The insight behind both was the same: In many cases, the downgraded option was actually preferrable. A perfect example of this comes from the agricultural sector, where a growing number of John Deere tractors have smart integrated weather data and software—but take far longer to fix when they break down.

For example, while global sales of smartphones increased by just 2 percent in 2017, sales of "dumb phones," the simple phones without apps or Internet access, rose by 5 percent. In some cases, these featureless phones were sought by people looking to cure their smart phone addiction. In other cases, the growth came from people frustrated by the downsides of smart phones, such as the batteries that barely making it through a day of use.

Similarly, many people are dumping their wearable devices, with some reports estimating that a third of people who buy wearable fitness trackers stop using them within six months. Users realize quickly that the data they are generating have limited usefulness.

People are reverting to more basic technology not only because they are overwhelmed by sophisticated versions, but also because they fear that advanced technology can make us vulnerable to tampering and manipulation. In April 2018, computer science/engineering professor Alex Halderman at the University of Michigan posted a video showing how easy it was to hack an electronic voting machine. As a small audience watched, he infected the machine with malware that guaranteed a particular result no matter how the votes came in.

This potential for the political process and elections to be hacked is a global concern, and it has become particularly urgent since proof of Russian interference in the 2016 U.S. presidential elections came to light. That fear has led many to call for a decidedly low-tech solution: a return to paper ballots. As Halderman told the *Atlanta Journal-Constitution*, "Voting is not as safe as it needs to be. The safest technology is to have voters vote on a piece of paper."

Suspecting that technology is making our way of life vulnerable to attack, we are not only reverting to more basic tech, but also turning to products and brands that remind us of simpler times.

BACK TO THE BRANDS WE TRUST

In October of 2019, an unexpected advertisement graced the back cover of *PhotoKlassik International*, a German film photography magazine. The ad featured an illustration of a family driving through old tourist spots from the 1960s along with the tagline: "Add a special ingredient to your days out . . . Shoot film, and relive your memories for generations!"

The surprising company behind the ad was Kodak, which has spent the better part of the past decade quietly reminding people it still exists.

After 131 years in business, Eastman Kodak declared bankruptcy in 2012. The company's demise became a cautionary tale of the dangers of business short-sightedness. Although legend has it that a Kodak engineer named Steve Sasson invented the digital camera in the 1970s, the company failed to embrace digital photography, choosing instead to protect its core business: selling film. Today the brand is a shadow of its former self. Annual revenues have plummeted nearly 90 percent since 1990. And Kodak has reduced its workforce by more than 100,000 employees during the past decade.

Yet despite its decline and widely assumed death, Kodak is experiencing a minor resurgence.

For those of us who grew up before the rise of all things digital, Kodak is part of our history. We still remember buying Kodak film and trusting it to help us record and relive life's most important moments. The Kodak logo even appears on the back of many of our old printed photos, underscoring the fact that the brand is literally stamped on our memories.

Since 2017, Kodak has been capitalizing on the growing desire for more analog experiences, as well as our good will for the brand by marketing its heritage and analog products heavily. It has relaunched its iconic Super 8 cameras, resumed production of its Ektachrome film for diehard enthusiasts, launched a print magazine called *Kodachrome* to celebrate "analog culture," and partnered with a fashion retailer on a line of retro streetwear featuring its brand logo.

Kodak's return is just one of many such stories playing out across industries as skeptical consumers increasingly turn to brands they remember from their past.

Across the world from Buenos Aires, Argentina, to Edmonton, Canada, there has been a significant growth in "barcades," retro arcades that serve alcohol and food, as 30- and 40-somethings try to reconnect with their past by playing games from their youth. Also tapping this shift, video game manufacturers such as Sony, Nintendo, and Sega have all released classic gaming systems, bringing back interfaces and games from the 1980s and '90s. Most have been wildly popular. When the Nintendo Entertainment System Classic with thirty preloaded games initially was released, for example, the $60 console sold out immediately and then appeared for resale on eBay for hundreds of dollars.

Our powerful fascination with the past is infiltrating the entertainment industry as well. Popular movie franchises such as *Jurassic Park*, *Toy Story*, and *The Matrix* have announced or added new sequels. In addition, many actors are coming back to play the roles that defined them. Sir Patrick Stewart is reprising his role as Captain Jean-Luc Picard in a new *Star Trek* series. Harrison Ford has returned to his iconic portrayals of *Star Wars*' Han Solo, Indiana Jones, and *Blade Runner*'s Rick Deckard.

In a world that overwhelms us with so many choices, we are turning back the clock to the movie franchises, products, and games that we remember and love — and more important, that we know won't disappoint us.

THE CONTINUING APPEAL OF ARTISAN CRAFTS

This same shift is leading consumers to seek things that were made the old-fashioned way and will therefore stand the test of time: artisanal products and traditional crafts. Buying these products offers a more meaningful and valuable purchasing experience as well as an antidote to our consumption of cheap disposable items.

Consider, for example, the world's best umbrella, which is only sold from a tiny workshop in Naples, Italy, where generations of craftsmen from the Talarico family have made umbrellas for more than 150 years. These umbrellas are hand-carved from local Italian wood by Mario Talarico and his nephew, an apprentice. Each one takes seven hours to make. The shop sells only 220 umbrellas a year for the approachable price of 200 euros each.

A few hours' drive away, in the Swiss city of Neuchâtel, there is a workshop plus chateau owned by a man who might be described as the best watchmaker in the world. Kari Voutilainen has earned five top prizes at the Grand Prix d'Horlogerie Genève, the Oscars of watchmaking. He produces about 50 watches each year, and his customers routinely pay anywhere from $75,000 up to $500,000 for his creations.

There are a shrinking number of such artisans across the world making widely beloved products, but they are getting harder and harder to find.

The beautiful objects that these artisans create are steeped in history, tradition, and lore. When we buy them, we feel connected to the past. They take us back to a time when we purchased products handmade by someone we knew, not from a faceless corporate conglomerate or an online store. They are products we can trust precisely because we buy them directly from the person who made them.

Our love affair with artisanal crafts is not only about our desire to connect with products from the past, but also our eagerness to connect with how things were done in the past and how we related to one another.

DIGITAL CONSERVATION AND BRANDED HISTORY

The final element of this megatrend has less to do with the things we buy and more to do with our increasing desire to preserve and learn from the past to cope with our complex present. We are worried that as technology becomes more sophisticated, and we race toward a future we imagined possible only in science fiction, we are leaving too much of our past behind. This fear is manifesting itself in the increasing number of efforts to preserve our past, often in digital form.

In September of 2018 a devastating fire ravaged the 200-year-old National Museum in Brazil. Several years earlier a more intentional destruction of historical artifacts in Iraq and Syria. Both point to a sad reality of cultural destruction and historical devastation that seem impossible to prevent. While we may not be able to anticipate or fight back against such disasters, teams of "digital conservators" have started initiatives over the past decade to use a combination of technology including 3D scanners, satellite imagery, drone mapping. Small armies of tech-savvy young people are being dispatched to take photos of historical landmarks to preserve their memory before the unthinkable happens.

The desire to save and remember the present has been around for most of recorded human history. In the past 100 years we have gotten far more visual with this desire, thanks to photography and video, The beautiful side effect is that these initiatives also are making the past easier to experience and access on demand, often alongside the present.

This is the final piece of the *Revivalism* megatrend and a sobering reminder that alongside the pleasantly nostalgic experiences of playing a board game or buying an artisan-made umbrella is the very real and urgent need to find better ways to preserve and protect the past both for ourselves and for future generations.

REVIVALISM AT A GLANCE

Above all, the *Revivalism* megatrend describes our widespread desire to revert to simpler times as a coping mechanism for our increasingly fast-moving world. Fueled by nostalgia and our penchant for romanticizing the past, we seek artisanal products, more basic technologies, and historic brands that stood the test of time. In short, we are looking for cultural reminders of that simpler time in a bid to recreate it for ourselves in the present.

Although we gravitate to the past and physical things from it, the irony is that we are using technology to preserve those very artifacts before they disappear entirely. The *Revivalism* megatrend is as much about reviving the past as it is about preserving it.

1. SHARE YOUR HISTORY.

Whenever possible, preserve and catalog your company's history. One way to do so is to capture your employees' stories about working at your company, building its products, and marketing them. These stories can offer a wealth of content that not only increases engagement with consumers but also yields company lore that contributes to culture building, recruiting and training efforts, and marketing and PR.

2. OFFER A CLASSIC MODE.

Sometimes consumers want to downgrade the functionality in the products they buy. The best companies offer an easy way to do that. For example, whenever Microsoft launches a new operating system, it allows users to revert the interface to a classic view, one from the previous version they were used to. The newest Samsung Galaxy mobile phone allows you to switch to an ultra power-saving mode, which turns off almost all functionality except calling, quickly "dumbing down" your phone to save the battery. Find ways to offer a classic mode for your products or services.

3. MAKE YOUR EXPERIENCE COLLECTIBLE.

Part of the appeal of tactile products such as physical books or art comes from the human desire to collect things. We enjoy the sense of achievement when we complete a collection or add meaningful pieces to it. It is the reason that we love getting another stamp in our passports at immigration, or why we like buying products in sets rather than individually. Consider the aspects of your customer experience that you might be able to make collectible in print, so customers come back again and again to collect them.

THE EVOLUTION OF REVIVALISM

A review of past trends that relate to this Megatrend:

PRECIOUS PRINT (2013 + 2017)

As a result of the digital revolution, people place more value on physical objects in print.

STRATEGIC DOWNGRADING (2016)

Consumers selectively skip upgraded versions and opt for simpler, cheaper, and sometimes more functional versions instead.

PRESERVED PAST (2017)

Technology is offering new ways to preserve history, changing the way we learn from, experience, and remember the past in the process.

DESPERATE DETOX (2017)

As technology, media clutter, and an overload of gadgets make life increasingly stressful, people are seeking moments of reflection and pause.

TOUCHWORTHY (2018)

Overwhelmed by digital and tired of sitting behind a screen, consumers are seeking products and experiences that they can touch and feel.

DELIBERATE DOWNGRADING (2019)

As tech-enabled products become overbearing, consumers opt to downgrade to simpler, cheaper, or more functional versions instead.

RETROTRUST (2019)

Often unsure of whom to trust, today's consumers are connecting with brands that have a rich legacy in cultural history, or those for which they have a strong sense of nostalgia.

REVIVALISM

08 HUMAN MODE

WHAT'S THE MEGATREND?

Tired of technology that isolates us from one another, people seek out and place greater value on physical, authentic and "unperfect" experiences designed with empathy and delivered by humans.

WHEN THE UNITED STATES WAS MIRED in its financial crisis of 2008, a small group of technologists created the "robo-advisor," an automated tool that delivers financial planning advice based on algorithms. The tool essentially removed the need for clients to interact with financial advisors and their potential bias and self-interest. Two years later, entrepreneur Jon Stein created Betterment, a robo-advisory platform based on this tool, which quickly grew to serve more than 300,000 customers and manage $16.4 billion in assets. A decade later, Betterment made an announcement that surprised many in the financial community: It added a human option. In exchange for an increased fee on assets under management, customers would have unlimited access to a real-life financial advisor. Why would one of the leading proponents of automated financial services reverse course and offer human advice as a premium? It turns out that for certain aspects of our lives and despite the opportunity for automation, we still prefer to deal with real people.

In many industries, human-led customer interaction is being replaced by automated technologies to cut costs and increase efficiency. Retailers are experimenting with cashier-free checkout kiosks. Brands are delivering customer service through artificially intelligent chatbots. And innovations in drone technology and self-driving trucks seem to point to a future of fully automated home delivery.

A recent report from McKinsey estimated that 45 percent of the activities that people currently are paid to perform might be automated in the future. Yet even as this automation revolution happens, there are signs that it is creating a resurgence in the value of and need for a more human option that often involves interactions with real people who are compassionate and skilled. As this preference grows, brands are responding by putting a more personal touch on their products and services to show their humanity and delight their customers.

This is the *Human Mode*, a megatrend we believe has been building for years. When I published the first trend report in 2011, I wrote about the growing number of organizations featuring employees and their amazing stories in marketing, a trend my team called *Employees as Heroes*. A year later, we identified the *Corporate Humanism* trend: how corporations were trying to be more transparent and show a human side. In 2014, we described how the most human stories online were often the ones shared the most virally, a trend we named *Shareable Humanity*.

These trends share a consistent theme: In a world booming with technology, there are signs that our humanity matters more than ever before.

AUTHENTICITY IN A FAKE WORLD

To illustrate this shift, let's consider the luxury sector. The fact that consumers increasingly want to spend money on experiences rather than products is urging a reevaluation of what makes a product a luxury. In 2018 we observed that luxury experiences are becoming less about exclusivity and extravagance and more about how authentically human they are or the story they offer — a trend we named *Approachable Luxury*.

One brand that exemplifies this trend is Shinola, a leather goods retailer that *Adweek* magazine once described as "the coolest brand in America." The Detroit-based company has grown to thirty-one stores across the United States and in London over nine years. Its huge success is due in part to leveraging its "Made in Detroit" story focusing on its commitment to setting up shop in a city that many businesses had abandoned. Shinola's origin story plus a touch of nostalgia for old-fashioned, crafted leather goods have won the hearts of consumers looking for authenticity.

Customers who buy a Shinola product know that they also are helping to rebuild one of America's most storied cities. Shinola might charge $500 for a watch, but it's made in the Motor City, a decidedly down-to-earth place, rather than in Switzerland. It feels more authentic to its largely American consumer base.

Shinola's story shows that consumers are asking how much humanity and authenticity a brand has before deciding whether it is worth buying or investing their time. One of the more curious examples of this preference for authenticity is the viral popularity of Korean *mukbang* shows, where thousands of viewers tune in to watch a stranger eat a hefty meal on video. Some suggest that these shows are popular thanks to female fans on a diet who get a vicarious thrill watching a stranger devour multiple meals in a sitting. Others think that the popularity of the videos reflects a deeper desire for something real in our fake world, especially online. There's plenty of evidence to make this case.

IN PRAISE OF VULNERABILITY AND UNPERFECTION

Although it's easy to think that social media rely mostly on frivolous content, plenty of genuine moments of humanity are mixed in with the silliness. People not only are embracing vulnerability online, but also are sharing the sad, insecure, turbulent, or other imperfect moments in their lives with their friends, families, followers, and even perfect strangers. In fact, the currency today isn't perfection but rather what I called *Unperfection* in a trend of the same name: the combination of vulnerability and authenticity.

Anna Akana's YouTube channel, with more than 300 million views, might seem a lot like those of other aspiring actresses and musicians. She features cute videos about her workout routine and empowering segments targeted at her young female audience. But her most popular video is nearly ten years old and not like the others. It's titled "Please Don't Kill Yourself." In four minutes and forty-four seconds of direct-to-camera video, Akana shares what she and her family went through after her sister committed suicide. Through tears, she pleads with viewers not to do the same to their loved ones. It's heartbreakingly raw and has deservedly gone viral.

In another widely seen example, comedian Amy Schumer demonstrated her unperfection by posing partially nude in a calendar photo shoot, and then posting the following message on social media: "Beautiful, gross, strong, thin, fat, pretty, ugly, sexy, disgusting, flawless, woman. Thank you @annieleibovitz." Her experience illustrates the reality of how celebrities are winning fans by being open about themselves. It is also a sign of how the entertainment and fashion industries, long criticized for perpetuating unrealistic body standards, are shifting toward valuing imperfections.

In May 2017, *Elle* magazine's cover featured Winnie Harlow, a model with vitiligo, which makes parts of her skin appear white due to loss of pigmentation. Many brands are using more realistic models in advertising, and several even signed a "No Photoshop" pledge to avoid excessive picture retouching.

Seeing more of one another's flaws is bringing out more empathy and understanding. It's also making us more receptive to brands that help us act with empathy and offer it to use in their products and services as well.

BRANDS INVEST IN EMPATHY

In January 2017, United Kingdom-based grocery giant Tesco purposefully created a slow checkout line at one of its Scotland stores. The elderly, those with physical disabilities or mental illnesses, and others who may need more time or employee assistance are often forgotten in the race to optimize retail for the masses. Tesco designed its "relaxed checkout" specifically for them.

We've seen many brands in recent years work to create similar experiences that cater to those who have been overlooked in the past. Starbucks, for example, opened a "sign language only" location in Washington, D.C., near the world-renowned Gallaudet University, which focuses on education of the deaf and hard of hearing. Microsoft, SAP, Ford, and other large organizations are all investing in initiatives to hire more neurodiverse and differently abled people.

In Madrid, Spain, the Prado Museum displays six three-dimensional replicas of famous paintings so the visually impaired can experience these masterpieces through touch. U.S. fashion label Tommy Hilfiger launched a disability-friendly line of clothing, Tommy Adaptive, that includes items with easy magnetic closures and wide openings to fit over prosthetics.

All of these initiatives put empathy for workers and customers at the center of their experience instead of sidelining it as a nice-to-have project corporate social responsibility. More important, these efforts are allowing organizations to realize important business results, from driving a more loyal workforce to capturing attention from more demanding and empowered customers.

In some cases, this focus on empathy also is helping change how people fundamentally see the world and understand the experiences and mindsets of those unlike ourselves. Vienna's Magdas Hotel is a compelling example. The boutique hotel allows affluent travelers to live alongside young refugees. Launched by European nonprofit Caritas, the project offers a powerful way for people to empathize with an often-overlooked group.

VIRTUAL EMPATHY

Virtual reality (VR) delivers immersive content that transports us into simulated versions of often unfamiliar situations. It allows us to put ourselves in the shoes of those who might differ from us, such as those who live in deep poverty or under threat of war. It also helps us better appreciate our environment. It might even make us more human.

Clouds over Sidra, a powerful VR film from producer Chris Milk, allowed participants to experience the stark, daily reality of Syrian refugees through the eyes of Sidra, a twelve-year-old girl. In *1,000 Cut Journey*, viewers experience being a young black man facing racism from fellow students or police officers. And a project from the *Guardian*, a UK-based newspaper, lets viewers feel what it is like to be a prisoner placed in solitary confinement. These content creations are examples of *Virtual Empathy*, a trend I've followed since we coined the term in 2016. As Milk famously stated in a 2015 TED Talk, VR is "the world's greatest empathy machine," with the potential to help us better understand others.

As the quality of VR continues to improve, so will its ability to engage. This will drive more widespread use of the technology beyond engaging entertainment experiences. Already it is being used in product manufacturing to better understand consumer needs, in education to shape how we learn, and in other ways to help extend our empathy.

THE DESPERATION OF LONELINESS

Perhaps nowhere else is the human value of empathy more apparent than in the considerable creativity applied by entrepreneurs to alleviate the sad exponential growth of loneliness across the globe.

Technology is not entirely to blame for this rise. In some cases, the loneliness is a result of people working in highly solitary jobs, such as truck drivers. In other cases, it may be the natural result of time as loved ones pass away, and those left behind struggle to continue life on their own. The loneliness can feel so crippling that some people are turning to unusual alternatives to fight it.

Some even resort to petty crime. In Japan, for example, 20 percent of all female prisoners are older than sixty-five. Many are incarcerated for crimes such as shoplifting that they committed intentionally in order to be detained. "I enjoy my life in prison more," one admits. "There are always people around, and I don't feel lonely here. . . . I don't have anything to look forward to outside."

This is the kind of story we hear about loneliness: despair mixed with desperation. In many cases, the loneliness coincides with aging and the loss of social and family networks that were part of our earlier life. In part, it is the result of the mathematics of longevity. As we live longer, there are fewer young people to care for our aging selves. Some cultures, such as Japan are already feeling these effects, and the rest of the world soon will face this demographic reality. In the United States alone, older people are projected to out-number children by the year 2030.

How we will take care of our aging populations and ensure their quality of life is becoming particularly urgent because, according to AARP, nearly 90 percent of people older than sixty-five prefer to age at home. There is ample medical evidence to suggest that if they do, they might have better health as well. But family members often can't take care of elderly relatives at home or hire someone to help them, so a host of problems, including loneliness, can set in.

In an ironic twist, technology may help us find a human solution to this problem.

ROBOPETS AND DIGITAL AVATARS

Another lonely category from Japan consists of salarymen who work long hours at the office and have no family. For companionship, a company called Gatebox has created a "holographic wife" virtual assis-tant, which is offered along with a monthly subscription. The holo-gram greets you when you come home from work, wakes you up, and even can send text messages throughout the day just to check in.

If that seems extreme, let's consider the story of Jibo, designed to be the world's friendliest robot. When Jibo first launched in late 2017, early customers loved him. *TIME* magazine even declared Jibo one of the best inventions of the year and put him on the cover. Sadly, less than a year later, the company behind Jibo ceased oper-ations. So his servers may go offline at any moment.

The loss of Jibo, according to one account, was like the loss of a family member. Such was the deep emotional attachment that could happen with a well-designed robot. The connection can be even deeper when it happens with a digital avatar that has a real person behind it.

A start-up called care.coach offers a digital avatar, usually in the shape of a cute animated pet, that appears on a tablet screen and inter-acts with clients. This avatar reminds clients to take medications, drink water so they stay hydrated, and go to their next doctor appointment. In fact, the avatar is a real staffer who operates the avatar's voice behind the scenes. The tablet has one-way video enabled so care.coach team members can keep an eye on clients. If they see the person fall or believe he or she needs medical attention, they can call for help quickly. More important, care.coach team members engage with their clients in a meaningful way, encouraging them to share memories, listening to their stories, reading to them, and offering companionship.

For clients, the avatar becomes like a cross between a pet and a friend, continually checking on them and helping them with whatever they need. Care.coach's deeply personalized service works because it not only responds to basic care needs but also considers emotional needs. It offers empathy with clients' desire to live in a familiar, safe place and to talk to someone who understands them.

HUMAN MODE AT A GLANCE

The growth of automation is having a pronounced side effect: Human experiences are more desirable and valuable. We crave face-to-face interactions, and we trust personalities, brands, and products that seem authentic because they own their imperfections. Often blamed as a dehumanizing force, technology is offering new and tangible ways to have more human experiences through interacting with lifelike holograms and robots, engaging with real people through digital avatars, and experiencing empathy-creating experiences through virtual reality.

These innovations will dramatically change how we care for the aging as well as help anyone manage loneliness and the need for companionship. At the same time, there is a danger that human contact may increasingly be seen (and sold) as a luxury item and therefore available only to those with the financial means to pay for it. In the future this tension between the need for human experiences and the cost of making those experiences available to all who want or need them will become a major source of friction as well as opportunity.

HOW TO USE HUMAN MODE

1. COMMUNICATE IN HUMAN WAYS.

Insensitive phrases are all too common and used in business without a second thought, but they can be easily misinterpreted by people unfamiliar with them. I once saw a business leader promise he was telling the truth by saying there was no intent to "obfuscate." It is hard to trust a leader who uses a word like that. In the future, organizations and leaders that engender the most trust will be those that systematically eliminate business jargon and communicate in more human ways.

2. INNOVATE FOR HUMANITY, NOT FOR SPEED.

The word *innovation* often is used synonymously with *technology*, especially when upgrading technology to the next level. However, innovation is actually about finding new ways to do things, and sometimes the best innovation is to focus on improving the humanity of an experience rather than making it faster or cheaper. Just as the relaxed checkout line at Tesco reimagines the grocery visit with more empathy, you can rethink your experiences to bring more humanity.

3. EMBRACE "UNPERFECTION."

Do you think that the Tower of Pisa would have become an enduring tourist attraction if it hadn't been leaning? Flawed things are appealing because their imperfections make them seem more authentic. This translates into an important lesson, whether we are considering using this idea for business or ourselves. Sharing your imperfections can offer an authentic and believable reason for someone to trust you because you are demonstrating honesty and vulnerability. Being flawed makes you more human, and in an increasing number of situations, that is what matters most.

THE EVOLUTION OF HUMAN MODE

A review of past trends that relate to this Megatrend:

LIKEONOMICS (2011)
Influencers lend social capital to brands,
helping the most human brands win.

↓

APPROACHABLE CELEBRITY (2011)
Social media allow direct access to
previously unreachable celebrities.

↓

EMPLOYEES AS HEROES (2011)
Large and small brands demonstrate humanity
by featuring employee stories.

↓

CORPORATE HUMANISM (2012)
Companies find more ways to avoid being
faceless and show their humanity.

↓

SHAREABLE HUMANITY (2014)
Content shared on social media gets more emotional
as people share amazing examples of humanity and brands
inject more into their marketing communications efforts.

↓

VIRTUAL EMPATHY (2016 + 2018)
A rise in virtual reality experiences will lead to greater
human and corporate empathy thanks to the immersive
ability to see the world through unfamiliar eyes.

↓

APPROACHABLE LUXURY (2018)
Luxury is no longer defined by scarcity and privilege,
but rather through more down-to-earth human experiences
that create unforgettable moments worth sharing.

↓

continued ➡

(LOVABLE) UNPERFECTION (2014, 2015 + 2017)

As people seek more personal and human experiences, brands and creators intentionally focus on using personality, quirkiness, and intentional imperfections to make their products and experiences more authentic and desirable.

HUMAN MODE (2018)

As automation increases, people hungry for more personal and authentic experiences begin to put a premium on advice, services, and interaction involving other people.

ENTERPRISE EMPATHY (2019)

Empathy becomes a driver of innovation and revenue and a point of differentiation for products, services, hiring, and experiences.

↓

HUMAN MODE

09 ATTENTION WEALTH

WHAT'S THE MEGATREND?

In the information economy, our attention is our most valuable resource, leading us to be more skeptical of those who manipulate us to get it, and instead seek out and trust those who communicate in more authentic ways.

THE FIRST TIME I WAS INVITED to speak at the popular South by Southwest Festival (SXSW) in Texas, I made the mistake of checking the program to see how many other sessions were scheduled the same time slot: twenty-seven. Luckily I knew the event would have plenty of attendees, so my problem wasn't going to be getting people to show up. Instead, the real challenge was keeping their attention while they were sitting in my room thinking about all the other sessions they were missing.

The fear of missing out (FOMO) can be a powerful emotion. At SXSW, attendees at one session have been known to get up and leave if social media explodes with comments raving about another concurrent session nearby. Thankfully, my talk didn't elicit a mass exodus, but I heard it happened to several other speakers.

A few weeks after the event, I wrote an article suggesting that perhaps SXSW had become the ultimate example of always missing out: No matter what you did or where you went, you were sure to miss at least 95 percent of everything else. There was a hard cost to attending any session: the real-time reminders of all the others you chose to skip. No one was truly present, which meant everyone missed 100 percent of the experience both in their room and elsewhere and in the room they were in.

Sadly, this is a problem that we seem to encounter daily. We're bombarded with so many choices to invest our attention that the decision can be paralyzing. It doesn't help that credible reports show our attention spans are getting shorter. Although we have the ability to focus for a limited time, the noise surrounding us has made that more difficult. Our attention is becoming more selective and less easy to attract.

At the same time, our attention continues to be extremely valuable to organizations, brands, politicians, and even our own network of friends and colleagues. This is a world driven by *Attention Wealth*, our term for a megatrend that describes our information-driven society. Here the greatest political, financial and societal influence belongs to those who can best attract our attention. As a result of this reality, the competition for our attention wealth has evolved into a full-fledged war among those who hope to monetize it or leverage it to consolidate their power. The effects of this battle can be seen in almost every corner of our culture.

Brands create bigger spectacles to promote themselves and their products. Sensationalized headlines on news sites pose irresistible temptations for click-baiting. Politicians gain popularity by sending outrageous tweets that demand attention like a badly mangled car crash on the side of the road.

Those who are winning the battle for our attention are the ones who choose to assault it through shock or awe. Perhaps predictably, their grandstanding has made us *more* skeptical of the world in general, more selective about whom we trust, and more distractible from anything that does manage to capture our attention momentarily. In response, the spectacles they design to capture our attention are getting bigger and bigger.

THE AGE OF SPECTACLE

Flugtag is perhaps the world's largest annual gathering of people intent on watching predictable failure. Teams compete to build and launch a human-powered machine that will fly as far as possible before landing unceremoniously in the water beneath the launch platform. Most contraptions crash almost immediately.

The event is one of many spectacles sponsored by the energy drink brand Red Bull. More than most other brands, Red Bull has figured out how to monetize spectacle. The brand hosts an extreme mountain biking event and famously orchestrated the world's longest supersonic free fall — an event that millions of people watched happen live online. During the past decade, the brand has built a media empire that includes television programming, a popular magazine, and dozens of signature events and stunts.

In the process, Red Bull is the blueprint for hundreds of other brands hoping to become similarly adept at attracting and profiting from our attention wealth. There are plenty of entertaining, strange, and sometimes over-the-top examples.

For example, Frito-Lay launched a Cheetos Museum both online and inside the Times Square location of *Ripley's Believe It or Not*. The venue features famously shaped Cheetos submitted by customers, including "Cheesebraham Lincoln" and the "Locheese Monster." The venue follows a template established by pop-up art installations such as the Museum of Ice Cream, which features whimsical ice-cream-themed exhibits, and Candytopia, a "sugary spectacle" that offers a dozen interactive installations, including a marshmallow pit. As I was putting the finishing touches on this book, on a visit to our local shopping mall I even passed a Halloween Selfie Museum, where you can pay to take photos of yourself with gruesome Halloween creations.

These installations deliver the perfect setting for the ultimate selfie, delighting visitors with ever more colorful, exciting, Instagram-worthy spectacles. They appeal to our desire to have a unique experience, ironically by taking the same photos and sharing the same spectacle as untold numbers of other people. In 2019 we described this trend and those groups taking advantage of it as leveraging a *Strategic Spectacle*. Since then we have seen growing examples of this technique.

RETAIL SPECTACLE

Retailers too have adopted the strategy to win customers' attention with awe-inspiring spectacles. Stores are transforming from places where customers can buy their products to places where customers can experience them. MartinPatrick3 has been doing that for more than a decade, going far beyond the traditional bounds of retail.

Housed in a 130-year-old warehouse on the hip outskirts of the Twin Cities in Minnesota, the store sells an unusual combination of products: furniture alongside stylish men's clothing and interior design services. MP3, as it is affectionately known, operates almost like a tiny city block, with a bar and a barber shop. What sets the store apart from so many others is that it delights customers from the moment they walk in by greeting repeat customers by name and surprising new and old customers alike with an unexpected variety of products and showman-like customer care.

As e-commerce has grown, leading brick-and-mortar retailers have long worried that consumers will visit them only for "show-rooming"— trying a product in store only to purchase it from a different online retailer such as Amazon. This fear was so palpable that one Australian store even started charging a "just-looking fee" for customers who entered a store and left without buying anything.

Over time, however, retailers have shifted their focus toward delivering more memorable and immersive multichannel experiences that grab customers' attention and then entice them to complete their purchase either in the store or online. This strategy is even offering a path for failed brands to reinvent themselves. A mere two years after filing for bankruptcy, for example, retailer Toys 'R' Us announced in 2019 that it would launch a series of experiential stores where kids can "run around in the aisles and play with new toys."

Even many digital-first brands that built their success by disrupting traditional retailers have started opening physical retail stores, including Warby Parker, Glossier and perhaps most notably, Amazon. Some of these efforts lean heavily toward spectacle. During the Summer Olympics in Rio de Janeiro, Brazil, Samsung's Galaxy Hub custom Olympics-branded phones and collectible prizes. Online mattress retailer Casper created the Dreamery, a venue that offers nap sessions by appointment for busy Manhattanites.

Each of these experiences leverages the most reliable tactic for securing attention wealth: storytelling.

THE ART OF STORYTELLING

A recurring trend from several past reports is the idea of *Backstory-telling*, which I have been writing about and teaching for more than a decade. For the past 15 years as a strategist and speaker, I've been a passionate ambassador for the importance of brand storytelling. I have created and taught a graduate-level course in business story-telling at Georgetown University. Stories are a powerful tool because the human brain is more inclined to pay attention to an engaging narrative than to a bunch of facts. Knowing this, brands are trying to win our attention and earn our trust by sharing their back stories and vulnerabilities. Huda Kattan is a good example.

The Iraqi American makeup artist, entrepreneur, and social media personality is fond of describing herself as "everyone's beauty BFF." In her case, that's not far from the truth: She has more than 40 million followers on Instagram, has been named one of the Internet's most influential people by *Time* magazine, and owns a rapidly expanding beauty empire under the brand Huda Beauty.

Based in Dubai, Kattan keeps her fans engaged by answering their questions on her blog and starring in video tutorials demon-strating how to use her latest products. By making herself the approachable "best friend from next door" star of her own show, she's won the loyalty of her fans and turned them into customers of her self-branded line.

Big cosmetics companies are hungry for that kind of attention-grabbing power. In 2018 alone, there were 52 acquisitions in the beauty and personal-care industry, the most in a decade. The major-ity of these smaller players were not acquired for their products, which are typically easy to formulate, but for the attention wealth their founders have earned from their large and loyal fan base.

For every human influencer like Huda, there are a growing number of artificial influencers, some of whom inspire a similarly frenzied loyalty from their fans.

ARTIFICIAL INFLUENCE

Sixteen-year-old pop superstar Hatsune Miku has performed at sold-out concerts around the world, her singing videos have crossed the 100 million views mark, and she has been paid handsomely to endorse products. Yet her rapid rise to fame, enabled by social media, isn't the most interesting thing about her. What sets her apart is that she isn't human. Miku is an anime character, and since her popularity has soared, she has been invited to endorse products such as the Toyota Corolla and to perform at live concerts with human backups. She is even a spokesperson for the city of Sapporo, Japan, where she supposedly was born.

Miku is not the only one. Shudu is another example: a striking, dark-skinned "digital supermodel" created by Cameron-James Wilson, a London-based fashion photographer. After a digitally created photo of Shudu wearing Fenty Beauty's lipstick went viral, Wilson received offers to partner her with brands, which quickly made her more than a piece of digital art. Lil Miquela, another digitally created influencer with a large following on Instagram, was commissioned in early 2019 to star alongside real-life model Bella Hadid in a controversial Calvin Klein ad where the two share a racy kiss. The rise of these invented celebrities is a new approach to grab *Attention Wealth* and was a phenomenon we wrote about with our trend of *Artificial Influence* in 2019.

In many cases, artificial influencers like Miku, Shudu, or Lil Miquela succeed by attracting the highly desirable youth demographic — a notoriously hard-to-reach segment that brands are desperate to find new ways to engage. It makes sense, therefore, that these artificial influencers who seem to command an outsized audience from those skeptical young people should become magnets for brand sponsorship dollars.

As these artificial influencers are manicured to hold our attention, they are blurring the line between real and fake and making it incredibly difficult to know whom to trust. That trust is further tested by the disturbing rise of deepfakes—doctored videos or photos in which AI is used to superimpose a person's face on someone else's body to present a misleading scene.

DEEPFAKES AND ATTENTION SABOTAGE

In 2016, deepfakes gained notoriety from the global media when the technology was largely blamed for shifting the results of a presidential election in the Philippines. A series of fake videos showing presidential candidate Leila de Lima in a series of compromising sexual situations were circulated on Facebook and widely blamed for sabotaging her chances against Rodrigo Duterte, who went on to win.

Several months after the contentious Filipino election results, a team of researchers from the University of Chicago built a neural network that could write fake online restaurant reviews indistinguishable from those written by humans. Ben Zhao, one of the researchers, noted that technology like this has the potential to "shake our belief in what is real and what is not."

He is probably right. Technology that helps people or companies with self-serving intentions manufacture content that captures our attention and distorts the truth will continue to grow more sophisticated. As a result, we will become more skeptical of content in general, even that produced by seemingly legitimate fact-checked sources.

ATTENTION AND MANIPULATED OUTRAGE

In the first full quarter after Donald Trump's presidential victory in 2016, the *New York Times* reported the single biggest surge of subscribers in its history, adding more than 300,000 digital subscribers in less than a month. According to TV ratings data from Nielsen, cable news programming from Fox News, CNN, and MSNBC all saw double-digit ratings growth across the board for the second quarter of 2017. CNN had its most-watched first quarter in 14 years, and Fox News had the highest-rated quarter ever in cable news history.

According to some observers, the rise can be explained by the growth of a disturbing type of media that is often described as "outrage porn." The term refers to stories and headlines intentionally written in a way to provoke anger. It is a technique used frequently by liberal-leaning and conservative-leaning media outlets alike. When used effectively, it is nearly impossible to ignore. Outrage, in other words, has become a driver of profit in the news media industry because we can't help but pay attention.

Despite the many industry pronouncements that more focus is needed on facts and unbiased reporting, audiences are drawn to the hyperbolic reporting and commentary that are typical of cable news and reward those media with their attention.

When I first wrote about this effect in 2017, I called it *Manipulated Outrage*. The idea quickly became one of our most frequently discussed trends that year. Today we are faced with an explosion of *Manipulated Outrage* online, where stories are disseminated through social media by people who want to profit from or exploit our anger. We are exposed to routine sensationalism peddled by 24-hour news channels desperate to maintain a perpetual stream of supposedly important and urgent news. Lost in all this televised finger wagging is a shared sense of reality.

The good news is, there are signs that this cycle may be reaching its limit. As a result of the glut of sensationalism in media: people are becoming skeptical of what they read, hear, or see on every level. Every "breaking" news alert that desperately calls our immediate attention to something that is ultimately unimportant desensitizes us further. In his book *The Attention Merchants*, Tim Wu calls this the *disenchantment effect*. "When audiences begin to believe that they are being ill-used — whether overloaded, fooled, tricked, or purposefully manipulated," he explains, "the reaction can be severe and long-lasting enough to have serious commercial consequences and require a significant reinvention of approach."

When the world is supposedly on fire, why waste time worrying about it until you can smell smoke? Unfortunately, even when that smoke arrives, there are plenty of people who suggest it's just a smoke machine. I have referred to this state of affairs as our "modern believability crisis," when we are unsure of whom and what to believe or where to place our attention.

When that happens, we turn to the only source we feel we can truly trust: ourselves.

MORE INFORMED AND MORE NARROW MINDED

Surrounded by so much noise from brands, media outlets, and politicians vying for our attention and blurring the line between what's real or not, we've become good at selectively focusing out of necessity. To do so, we are turning inward to our core beliefs and aligning ourselves with those who share them. In the process, we are also becoming more closed off to perspectives that differ from our own, a trend we called *Truthing* back in 2018.

One of the effects of this introspective trend is that we are increasingly entrusting our attention to individual curators to help spotlight where we should spend our attention wealth. In some cases, these curators help inform us about what's going on in the world in a simplified and down-to-earth way — like speaking to a slightly opinionated but nonjudgmental older sibling who is always in the know.

One popular example is a curated daily newsletter called the *Daily Skimm*, from former TV news producers Danielle Weisberg and Carly Zakin. The newsletter appeals mainly to female millennials and reaches an audience of more than 7 million subscribers. For the past two years, I have aimed to provide a similar value for my readers by publishing my weekly *Non-Obvious Newsletter*, which curates the most interesting and underappreciated stories each week.

Unfortunately, sometimes our faith in these curators can be misplaced. That's easy to see from the popularity of most cable news talk-show hosts who generally thrive on inciting our outrage, categorizing opposing viewpoints as idiotic, and encouraging a more narrow-minded view of the world. When we get our news from these sources, we invite what *New York Times* writer Natasha Singer has dubbed an "online echo chamber," where personalization prevents us from being exposed to or learning from perspectives other than our own.

The rise of these one-sided manipulators presents a dangerous challenge to open-minded thinking, new ideas, and even democracy itself. In a world where it is possible to be both more informed and more narrow-minded at the same time, remaining a non-obvious thinker becomes a daily challenge.

ATTENTION WEALTH AT A GLANCE

In an information economy, attention is the currency. As reports of our shrinking attention spans increase, brands, the media, and politicians are engaging in an all-out war to capture attention any way they can. Only by capturing our attention can they monetize us — and so attention has become a new form of wealth. To win these battles, they are relying on shock, delight, or outrage as means to engage increasingly skeptical audiences. This constant noise is leading us to turn to trusted curators of information to help make sense of it all. Some are worthy of that trust, helping to decipher the noise, while others corrupt our attention with closed-minded sensationalism. At the same time, the battle for our attention is driving some to leverage technology for deploying artificial avatars, fabricating deepfakes, and inciting outrage as a way to distort our opinions and views.

As we each discover just how much wealth our attention contains, we will become more skeptical about who deserves it and who doesn't. In a world where we have more control over our attention wealth, we also have a responsibility to do our best to spend it wisely.

1. BEWARE OF SPECTACLE BACKLASH.

As the competition for attention intensifies, spectacles will continue to be deployed to attract attention. The truth is that some level of drama may be required to break through the noise, but getting someone to look up for a second isn't the same as truly engaging their attention. Further, if your organization and brand are not positioned to be "spectacle makers," it can result in a loss of credibility. The costs for disrespecting your audience's attention or failing to deliver what you promise will make it hard to earn attention in the future, no matter how much sensationalism you throw at them.

2. MAKE THE TRUTH MORE TRANSPARENT.

Every organization needs to find new ways to win consumers and audiences. This means finding the information sources your customers are most likely to trust and connecting with them. Seek out peer-to-peer validation, respected sources to provide a testimonial in your favor, or the right influencers who believe in your business and are willing to speak on its behalf.

3. SHARE YOUR BACK STORY.

To break through the noise, share your backstory, letting customers know why and how you do what you do. Luxury brand Hermès, for example, launched a film that takes consumers inside one of its silk mills in Lyon, France, to illustrate how its products are made. If you can share your story in an interesting way, showing your craft or trade with humility and vulnerability, you might be able to interest current customers or potentially new ones to spend more time (and money) with you.

THE EVOLUTION OF ATTENTION WEALTH

A review of past trends that relate to this Megatrend:

BRUTAL TRANSPARENCY (2011)

Aggressive honesty will lead to edgier and more effective marketing as brands reveal this unexpected tactic that consumers welcome.

CULTING OF RETAIL (2011)

The best retailers create passionate users who not only buy products but also rave about their experiences. They inspire those on their social networks to try the products themselves.

RETAIL THEATER (2012)

In the coming year, more retail stores will create unique experiences using the principles of theater to engage customers with memorable experiences.

BACKSTORYTELLING (2013 + 2018)

Organizations discover that taking people behind the scenes of their brand and history is one of the most powerful ways to inspire loyalty and drive purchase.

CURATED SENSATIONALISM (2014)

As the line between news and entertainment blurs, smart curation displaces journalism as engaging content is paired with sensational headlines to drive millions of views.

REVERSE RETAIL (2015)

Brands increasingly invest in high-touch, in-store experiences to build brand affinity and educate customers, while seamlessly integrating online channels to complete actual purchases and fulfill orders.

MANIPULATED OUTRAGE (2017)

Media, data analytics, and advertising are combining forces to create a perpetual stream of noise that is intended to incite rage and elicit angry reactions on social media and in real life.

continued ➜

TRUTHING (2018)

With trust eroding in media and institutions, people are engaging in a personal quest for the truth based on direct observation and face-to-face interaction.

ARTIFICIAL INFLUENCE (2019)

Creators, corporations, and governments use virtual creations to shift public perception, sell products, and even turn fantasy into reality.

STRATEGIC SPECTACLE (2019)

Brands and creators intentionally use spectacles to capture attention and drive engagement.

ATTENTION WEALTH

10 PURPOSEFUL PROFIT

WHAT'S THE MEGATREND?

As consumers and employees demand more sustainable and ethical practices from businesses, companies respond by adapting products, taking stands on issues, and putting purpose first.

TWENTY-FIVE YEARS AGO, Yvon Chouinard, founder of outdoor retailer Patagonia, wrote an essay titled "The Next Hundred Years," outlining his vision for the future.

Patagonia had been growing exponentially, and Chouinard was faced with a difficult choice: Sell the company and start a foundation for the environmental causes he championed or continue to build the brand. He decided to stick with the brand. "Perhaps the real good that we could do was to use the company as a tool for social change," he wrote, "as a model to show other companies that a company can do well by taking the long view and doing the right thing."

Patagonia has done both.

In the past decade alone, the brand has sued the U.S. government to reclaim public lands, donated millions of dollars of proceeds to environmental causes, pioneered the idea of "recommerce" by allowing customers to trade in used gear for credit, and published an interactive website where consumers can follow products from the production line all the way through shipment. In late 2018, Chouinard even rewrote the brand's mission statement to be more ambitious: "Patagonia is in business to save our home planet."

This militant stewardship of the Earth has been great for business, too. In the past seven years, Patagonia's revenue has quadrupled, surpassing a billion dollars annually while the brand continues to focus on social impact rather than growth.

Despite its success, for many years the brand was dismissed by the corporate world as a lonely outlier — evangelizing an appealing but unrealistic level of corporate altruism. Today the world has shifted. Rising consumer empowerment means people are flocking to buy from and work for brands that make a positive impact in the world. As a result, it is no longer enough for brands to focus on business as usual and measure success solely by financial growth. They are more frequently expected to step forward on social issues and stand up for their beliefs or risk losing both customers and employees. This is a megatrend we call *Purposeful Profit*, and it reflects a new business reality where companies are not only expected to do business in more ethical ways, but also they are finding that doing so pays off in tangible business results.

EMPOWERED CONSUMERS

In the past, consumers had limited information about how the products they bought were made. Sure, they could read ingredient lists on food, cosmetic, and cleaning products. But a curious consumer would quickly run out of sources information.

That is no longer the case. Thanks to the growing transparency of information on the Internet, consumers can learn about and shine a bright light on the practices of individual companies or entire industries. We now know about blood diamonds. The truth about the dangers of sugar and high-fructose corn syrup is common knowledge. In addition, companies have been forced to reveal how they use the data they collect about us online.

In many cases, smart entrepreneurs and organizations have created tools to make information about production processes and company behaviors actionable by offering consumers scorecards on brands, their products, workplace practices, and their own dealings.

Katariina Rantanen is one of those entrepreneurs. Her Helsinki-based team built an app that lets people instantly check the ingredients and ethical practices of cosmetic and beauty companies. Users simply scan the bar code of a product, and the tool, cleverly titled CosmEthics, pulls out data about how that product was made, whether it contains any banned ingredients, and whether it was tested on animals.

A startup bank, aptly called Aspiration, offers a checking account that automatically pulls data on the environmental and ethical practices of the brands you buy and calculates a personal impact assessment of your spending based on the published practices of the companies you are buying from. In 2019 a Swedish financial tech company called Doconomy released the world's first credit card with a carbon limit, which not only measures the carbon footprint of your consumption, but also cuts you off from any more purchases with the card once you reach your assigned limit.

Companies such as these are fueling the modern concept of voting with your wallet. As its popularity grows, additional consumer-empowerment apps will launch, helping consumers make more informed decisions in other industries as well.

VOCAL ABOUT VALUES

In 2018 we introduced a trend we called *Enlightened Consumption,* which suggested that consumers were increasingly seeing their choices about what they buy, where they work, and how they invest as meaningful expressions of their own values. Since then, we have seen these values personified by activist heroes such as sixteen-year-old Greta Thunberg, whose silent protests outside the Swedish Parliament building ignited a global movement of people mobilizing in support of the environment.

Though the movement was largely framed as an effort to get global government to act, there is a growing realization among consumers that they can also demand transparency from corporations and make an impact through the things they choose to buy or avoid.

For example, the backlash against genetically modified organisms (GMOs), high-fructose corn syrup, and artificial ingredients has led many of the world's largest brands, from McDonald's to Mars, to be more transparent about how their ingredients are sourced. The public also has declared war against the plastic straw, driving many restaurants to ban it.

Another way in which consumers are making their ethical stand known is with sustainable investing. The practice of purchasing stock in companies that consider social and environmental causes to bring about social change has been growing significantly. The Global Sustainable Investment Alliance, a group that aggregates data from around the world, measured growth in socially responsible investments of 34 percent to $30.7 trillion from 2017 to 2019. Data from Morgan Stanley's Institute for Sustainable Investing suggest that millennials are twice as likely as the general population to invest in companies or funds that target social or environmental outcomes.

This wave of consumer and investor interest in companies with sustainable social practices is spurring a corresponding shift in ethical company operations. Corporations are following consumers, just as Chouinard predicted.

BRANDS TAKE A STAND

One way companies are working harder to attract conscious consumers is by taking a stand for what they believe in. We first wrote about this trend, *Brand Stand*, in 2018. In the next decade, brands that bravely declare what they believe, choose to do good, and step up to protect people and the world around us in unexpected ways will continue to win the hearts of the public.

A watershed moment for this trend came in 2014 when CVS Health, the largest pharmacy chain in America, stopped selling tobacco products. At the time, analysts estimated the decision would cost the brand an estimated $2 billion a year in revenue. In 2019 CEO Larry Merlo credited that bold choice with reshaping the future of the company and perhaps the health care industry. In that five-year span, CVS has acquired a major health insurance company (Aetna), converted stores to become "health hubs," focused on health services and products, and nearly doubled its annual revenue in the process.

Sometimes brands make a stand more quietly. Deep inside one of the world's most famous factories, located in the tiny town of Billund, Denmark, more than a hundred engineers and scientists are collaborating to redesign a product that has worked perfectly for more than eighty years.

The LEGO Sustainable Materials Centre, a well-funded group within LEGO, is dedicated to finding more sustainable materials within the next decade to make the company's iconic bricks. In 2018 the group launched its first innovation, making flexible pieces such as leaves and palm trees from a plant-based plastic sourced from sugar cane.

This sense of commitment to the environment is deeply felt at LEGO. Its efforts may inspire more such initiatives across the toy industry, especially if consumers take note of LEGO's efforts and demand similar forward-looking commitments from other companies as well.

UNLIKELY SOCIAL CHANGE HEROES

Early in her career, English fashion designer Stella McCartney vowed never to use leather, fur, or feathers in her work. Animal rights activists and vocal vegetarians, however, rarely succeed in the world of luxury couture, where products are routinely made with animal products. Not surprisingly, her unorthodox choice initially was ridiculed within the industry.

But McCartney was undeterred. As she learned more about the destructive environmental impact of the fashion and textiles industry — which emits an estimated 1.2 billion tons of greenhouse gases annually — she set ambitious sustainability targets for her company. Her designs used organic cotton, recycled fibers, sustainably farmed wood, biodegradable plastic packaging, and of course, no leather or fur.

In the process, she became a heroine for customers who saw her as a crusader against the environmental impact of big fashion. Eventually, her success set off a movement in the industry that would have been unthinkable a decade ago. In 2017 rival luxury brands Gucci, Versace, Burberry, and several others announced their intentions to go fur-free as well.

This is a virtuous cycle. Companies choose to do good, consumers hail them as heroes, and other companies follow suit. And it all usually starts with a single visionary leader such as Stella McCartney or Yvon Chouinard.

The other effect of this cycle is that companies begin to demand more from the vendors they work with, fueling responsible innovation throughout their supply chain partners.

One interesting example of this effect comes from Robertson County, a small area in northern Tennessee that once was dominated by tobacco farms. Today those farmers mostly grow indigo plants thanks to entrepreneur Sarah Bellos and her company, Stony Creek Colors. Those vivid blue indigo plants are used to produce a natural blue dye that can replace the toxic synthetic dye that most denim manufacturers typically use. It is exactly the kind of innovation that sustainable designers like McCartney, and the empowered consumers who buy from her, are demanding.

LEADING AUDACIOUS CHANGE

Encouraged by consumers who support brands that take it upon themselves to be responsible citizens of the world, a slate of entrepreneurs like Bellos are developing similarly audacious plans to change the world with their startups — a trend we first curated in 2017 and described as *Moonshot Entrepreneurship*.

The concept of a "moonshot" that can change the world is easy to dismiss. To be sure, plenty of hubris and wishful thinking that fuels many such ideas, and they often fail. However, as the problems the world faces grow ever more urgent, the need for big solutions will require this kind of bold entrepreneurship. At the time of this writing, icebergs are melting, the Amazon forest is burning, and extreme weather dominates the global news cycle every week. In response, the world is increasingly ready to accept radical ideas from businesses, a trend we called *Good Speed* in 2019.

The Ocean Cleanup project is one example of how investors and others are supporting a wildly ambitious concept that many believed had no chance of success. The crazy idea came from a twenty-five-year-old Dutch entrepreneur named Boyan Slat, who dreamed up an idea to install huge floating barriers that could use the ocean's current to capture plastic waste from an area known as the Great Pacific Garbage Patch (an estimated 1.3 trillion items of plastic floating in the ocean between Hawaii and California).

The idea was hopelessly naïve and indeed did run into a series of problems when it first launched. But then in October of 2019, almost exactly seven years after first sharing his idea on stage at a TEDx conference, the system worked.

THE RISE OF *LIFTERS*

As we see more purposeful projects supported, they will often come from a more unlikely source: within corporations. As consumers and employees speak up for what matters to them, companies are responding. In 2015, we explored a trend we called *Mainstream Mindfulness* to describe a growing shift among companies investing in the power of mindfulness to inspire their workforce and solve bigger problems.

Two voices leading the connection between purpose, mindfulness and organizational performance are Dr. Eliza Shah and Paresh Shah, founders of Lifter Leadership. Their groundbreaking research has identified "Lifters," an emerging segment that spans all age groups and can be trained to drive purpose, innovation, workplace health and change. Lifters are positive, purposeful workers who simultaneously uplift their co-workers, customers, communities and their company. These initiatives are having a tangible business impact. According to business professor Raj Sisodia, organizations that adopt mindful, conscious practices, perform approximately ten times better than those who don't.

Ultimately, the organizations that lead with purpose will not only reinvent themselves by changing their products, doing good, and setting ambitious and purposeful world-changing goals that can also make our world a better place.

PURPOSEFUL PROFIT AT A GLANCE

In the past, brands would limit themselves to "soft branding" of cause-related initiatives — preferring to take a quiet role as an invisible supporter rather than taking a public stand. This was once the best way for a corporation to support initiatives that aligned with its core values without feeling overtly promotional.

Today brands are expected to be more vocal. Sitting on the sidelines is not enough. Now companies must work to earn consumers' trust through positive business models, ethical treatment of workers, charitable good deeds, socially responsible sourcing, and a daily commitment to purpose along *with* profit. Just as consumers are making intentional choices about what products to buy and brands to support, employees too are seeking workplaces that allow them to have a greater purpose and make a difference in the world.

1. TAKE A CREDIBLE POSITION.

As profit and purpose matter more than ever before, brands and leaders alike can fall into the trap of rushing to take a position or make a stand on an issue without thinking through whether others will see their move as credible. An example would be a financial services firm that decides to launch an initiative to support empowering female leaders within the company despite not having any women on their board of directors or in the C-suite. As consumers and employees regularly turn to organizations with a strong purpose, they will be more exacting of those who claim to have purpose but don't back up their words with actions.

2. FOCUS ON IMPACT.

The more real-time tools (such as barcode scanning apps and online reviews) that consumers have to instantly assess corporate practices, the more they will demand not only a commitment to doing good, but also to achieving results. Those who can show demonstrable positive impact on the world will be the ones who can inspire the most loyalty from customers and employees alike, and sustained returns for investors as well.

3. PRACTICE CONSCIOUS CAPITALISM.

On a more personal side, as consumers the power is in our hands. We may think that a small choice we make — perhaps forgoing a product that was produced questionably or paying a few dollars more for a product that was ethically made — doesn't really make a difference. After all, how much impact can one person have? Yet by making socially responsible choices consistently and thinking about the positive and negative impacts of our purchases, we can contribute to a ripple effect. With every decision about what we buy and where we buy it, we demonstrate what is important to us and send a clear message to organizations: the way they make their products and how they do business matters.

THE EVOLUTION OF PURPOSEFUL PROFIT

A review of past trends that relate to this Megatrend:

HEROIC DESIGN (2013)

Design takes a leading role in the introduction of new products, ideas, and campaigns to change the world.

↓

BRANDED BENEVOLENCE (2015)

Companies increasingly put brand purpose at the center of their organizations to show a deeper commitment to doing good as a part of business.

↓

MOONSHOT ENTREPRENEURSHIP (2017)

Our tendency to celebrate visionary entrepreneurs inspires a new generation of startup founders to think beyond profit and consider how their businesses can make a positive social impact and even save the world.

↓

BRAND STAND (2018)

Reacting to a polarized media atmosphere, more brands feel compelled to take a stand and highlight their core values rather than try to be all things to all people.

↓

ENLIGHTENED CONSUMPTION (2018)

Empowered with more information about products and services, people are choosing to make a statement about their values and the world today through what they buy, where they work, and how they invest.

↓

GOOD SPEED (2019)

The urgency of the problems facing humanity is inspiring corporations, entrepreneurs, and individuals to find ways of doing good (and generating results) faster.

↓

PURPOSEFUL PROFIT

11 DATA ABUNDANCE

WHAT'S THE MEGATREND?

The growing ubiquity of data and the myriad ways it can be collected raise big questions about how to make it truly useful, who owns the data, and who should stand to profit from it.

IN 1954 MANAGEMENT GURU Peter Drucker famously wrote, "What gets measured, gets managed."

For decades this mantra has described how the world sees data. Numbers are celebrated, and those who make decisions based on them are respected. The wealthiest companies in the world are the ones with access to the largest sets of data.

The unsurprising result of our data-reverent culture is that everyone is focused on finding new and better ways to amass more of it. Not only do companies constantly collect "big data" through the platforms they own, but our devices are generating perpetual streams of "small data" too. Voice-enabled devices are listening and recording conversations. Data from ride sharing apps, smart thermostats, streaming entertainment, online gaming, fitness trackers, and real-time traffic is all collected and stored, usually by those hoping to profit from the information.

Much of the small data comes from information we share willingly, because the implications of doing so rarely seem dangerous. Who cares if Netflix knows exactly which movies you choose to stream or Google knows that you are in the market for a new printer? In some ways, the fact that they have this information means they can create a better and more personalized experience for you.

Yet sometimes we are unwittingly sharing information that we don't intend. Uploading a photo online, for example, often includes hidden metadata such as an exact GPS location and time, which could be matched with photos from others to pinpoint who you were with and even what you were doing. The potential for misuse of facial tracking technology is so concerning that San Francisco and a handful of other cities have already banned its use.

In addition to all this data collected by organizations and information shared online by individuals, there is one other source of considerable data that is increasingly being made publicly available: "open data." This term refers to the vast stores of data dumped online by companies and governments in the name of transparency or regulatory compliance. The combination has created a haze of confusion that I described in 2018 with a trend we called *Data Pollution*. In the coming decade, this problem will get far worse.

By some expert estimates, a whopping 90 percent of the data that currently exists in the world was created in the past two years and it will continue to multiply exponentially.

This is the modern world of Data Abundance, where companies and consumers increasingly are generating and collecting ever expanding sets of data, prompting us to grapple with several key questions. How meaningful is all of this data? What should we do with all of it? Who should own the data? And perhaps most importantly, who should be allowed to profit from it?

GOOD DATA AND USELESS DATA

The agriculture industry, currently overrun by data, may offer some answers.

Today a single farm can provide mountains of data from sensors in the soil, wearable trackers on farm animals, and aerial drones for crop monitoring. This information enables precision farming—the ability to plant the right crop in the right spot and harvest it at the right time.

Some groups are combining the data from many sources in order to create something that provides value for the entire industry. The California-based Farmers Business Network is one example. The network asks farmers to share their data about chemical prices, field sizes, and crop yields. This information from thousands of participating farmers who collectively manage more than 22 million acres of farmland across the United States and Canada is input into a system so any member can see fair-market input prices, real-world seed performance, and optimal grain delivery points.

Similarly, open networks are popping up across other industries as well. In the medical field, for example, an app called Figure 1 has enlisted nearly 2.5 million medical professionals to share images of patients (with personal details removed) in order to help their peers diagnose difficult or rare conditions. Dubbed "Instagram for Doctors," the app has helped hundreds of professionals better treat their patients with the insights of colleagues around the world.

The proliferation of these open networks is proving extremely helpful to those who share in the data. However, that's true only when the data is good — up to date, clear, and manageable. More is not always better.

Vast data sets from governmental and non-governmental groups are being made available to others for use online. In theory, that may seem like a positive thing, but unfortunately, not all the data is usable. The GovLab Index, which tracks open data trends and publishes annual reports on the state of open data adoption by governments worldwide, revealed some sobering points:

- More than 1 million data sets have been made open by governments worldwide.

- Less than 7 percent of this data sets are published in both machine-readable forms and under open licenses.

- 96 percent of countries are sharing data sets that are not regularly updated.

When it comes to data, quality is far more important than quantity, as those who invest their advertisement dollars in social media platforms have learned.

FIVE TYPES OF DATA POLLUTION

DATA OVERFLOW	When too much data is captured, leaving organizations confused about what to focus on or prioritize.
DATA MANIPULATION	When the results and insights from data is twisted to support biased arguments.
DATA SABOTAGE	When people intentionally share incorrect or incomplete information with the intent to cause harm.
DATA CONTAMINATION	When data is collected from multiple sources, mixed together, and reclaimed or deleted by creators.
DATA EXPIRATION	When data is not updated as frequently as needed and therefore loses value because it is not current.

Originally published in the Non-Obvious 2018 Trend Report.

WHEN FAKE ACCOUNTS SPOIL THE DATA

Facebook has profited handsomely from the staggering amount of data it collects from users. To access the data, advertisers have flocked to Facebook. The volume of users and the details that Facebook knows about each of them offer advertisers a huge opportunity to target people specifically based on what they believe, who they listen to, what they like, and what they are searching for.

Other online platforms are offering a similar pitch to brands, but they are all facing a real and growing problem: Many of the users on their platforms are actually trolls, fake accounts or bots.

In the first six months of 2019, Facebook performed what is becoming a necessary ritual of purging fake accounts from its system. According to reports, the purge was its largest ever: It removed 3.39 billion fake accounts. The fake accounts, created in half a year, were more than Facebook's estimates of real accounts on the platform, which were about 2.4 billion.

It is hard to tell how many social media accounts might be fake because most platforms are reluctant to share those numbers publicly. However, some independent researchers estimate that at least 15 percent of all social media profiles may be autogenerated without a real person behind them. This high percentage of fakes is frustrating advertisers.

One person leading the charge to address this issue is Procter & Gamble's chief brand officer, Marc Pritchard. In 2017 he famously cut more than $200 million in digital ad spending due to concerns about viewability, fraud, and a lack of quality measurement. The move created a tidal wave within the media industry and set off a scramble to purge dead accounts and clean up their data.

Unfortunately, fake social media accounts are not the only way data has become polluted. Users themselves often contribute to compromised or missing data.

I follow my 15-year-old son on Instagram, and last month I noticed something strange on his account. After spending weeks traveling on the West Coast during the summer and sharing lots of images, his account was down to just four pictures of our trip. Worried that he had lost some of his content, I asked him about it.

"I deleted them," he told me.

"Why?" I asked him, puzzled by his answer.

"I didn't need them."

Most of my son's posts get about ten times as many likes as mine do, but that social proof doesn't seem to matter to him. While I use social media as a gallery of my life, he uses it as an article of clothing: something to be worn today and changed tomorrow. It turns out he's not alone.

A story in the *Washington Post* reported that teenagers are curating their accounts on Instagram and deleting old photos that either did not get many likes or no longer were wanted on their profiles. But when users delete old posts, that alters their page views and engagement time stats, skewing the data that Instagram is trying to monetize. The less accurate their data, the fewer opportunities there are to sell advertising. Desperate to stop users from deleting the data its business model depends on, Instagram introduced a feature that allows users to archive their old images instead of deleting them.

As we continue to generate more data, there will be growing urgency to ensure the data is in good enough shape to be usable. There is also a societal cost to our *Overquantified Life,* as I termed it in a trend from my 2014 report. In a world where all our online interactions can be reduced to a number, people might start to prioritize their numbers over everything else and rely on such figures to fuel their behavior. Any experience might seem worth sharing only if it generates the right social response from friends and strangers online.

If a tree falls in the forest, and there's no selfie of someone standing in front of it, how do we know it really happened?

To inspire people to escape this sad gamification of life experiences, Instagram is one platform leading a charge to hide likes from interactions altogether. The decision has been so popular that many other platforms are considering implementing the move as well.

Whether we see these numbers or not, the problem of what those numbers actually mean remains.

MAKING MEANING OUT OF DATA

Wearable fitness trackers have become incredibly popular in the past few years, with U.S. consumer use increasing from 9 percent in 2014 to 33 percent in 2018. These devices collect all sorts of health information, from heart rate to sleep patterns to exercise time, which health providers can use to determine the user's well-being.

But as Dr. Fred N. Pelzman of Weill Cornell Medicine suggests, health care providers often struggle to make sense of all the data. "Every morning when I log onto our electronic health record, one group of messages are from patients with their self-recorded health information data that they've sent to me for review," he writes in the popular medical blog KevinMD. "Looking at too much data creates too many possibilities. It could always be something."

In other words, having access to a treasure trove of data collected by wearable devices doesn't necessarily translate to health providers finding meaning in it. Even patients struggle to find real value in the data beyond "feel-good stats." The devices provide plenty of pats on the back, for example, displaying celebratory firework icons every time the user reaches an arbitrary goal, such as walking 10,000 steps in a day. The result is plenty of data collection, yet potentially little impact on long-term health or happiness from it.

This is a common struggle for small-scale data analysis, but what about large data sets that are far too complex for humans to analyze in the first place? In these cases most organizations rely on machine learning and artificial intelligence to automate the task of reviewing vast stores of data and instantly extrapolating useful insights.

Chinese insurance giant Ping An is a perfect example of the potential of this method. The company spent three years perfecting its AI-based Superfast Onsite Investigation claims system, which matches photos of vehicle damage against a database of 25 million parts used in 60,000 different makes and models of cars sold in China. It then calculates the cost of parts and labor to fix that damage in more than 140,000 garages across China. The system is augmented with facial recognition that reads consumer expressions to detect possible lying and potentially fraudulent claims. In its first year of operation, the online system reportedly helped the company settle more than 7 million claims and save more than $750 million.

As the amount of data collected soars, companies that can sort it out in a meaningful and timely way will be poised to reap major benefits. However, that's possible only as long as the information remains available to them. Sometimes it may not be.

DATA OWNERSHIP AND PROFITABLE DATA

The explosion of social media platforms and Internet-connected devices allows us to capture our every action and thought instantly. Most of this data is not solicited or traditionally owned by brands. As consumer-owned "small data" rivals brand-owned "big data," the most pressing question facing businesses in the coming years will be whether we do or don't choose to continue sharing our data with them as freely as we have.

Today the Internet is filled with websites that entice us to trade our personal information for some type of reward. Want to buy a ticket to an event or download a free report? Give us your email address. Need to register a product? Answer a short survey to acti-vate your warranty. Along with this form-collected data, the more time we spend browsing websites, adding products to our carts, or sharing and publishing opinions through social media, the more our information becomes part of the big data set that companies collect and use to market and customize product offers to us.

Although we willingly trade our data, we remain concerned about how such details are used, a point I wrote about back in 2014 with a trend we called *Privacy Paranoia*. Still, the reason we do it is because we are under the influence of what behavioral economics call *benefit immediacy*: We share information willingly because the benefits of doing so are immediate while the risks are delayed.

As we continue to use smart devices that collect enormous amount of data, we will shift from being the creators of data to the real-time consumers and owners of it. We will be able to unlock the data we created from the platforms that collected it — seemingly innocuous products such as wi-fi tea kettles and mood-tracking bracelets — and will be in a position to share it with those who offer us the right incentives to do so.

In this world consumers will benefit directly from *Data Abun-dance* in a new way. As personal data begins to deliver individual profit, the balance again will shift between what people are willing to share and how deeply they are willing to allow data collection to enter their lives. Unfortunately, sometimes they won't have a choice.

SOCIAL CREDIT AND RATINGS

In late 2018, Uber introduced a societal cost for being a jerk.

For more than a decade, the idea of ratings has been a one-way interaction. There are platforms for rating retailers, restaurants, doctors, and teachers — and they all share the same basic assumption: The consumer is the one who provides the rating. Consumers have begun to trust these ratings so explicitly that in many cases restaurants might go out of business and products might languish on shelves solely because of low ratings online.

What if those ratings could be applied the other way around? Uber and other ride-sharing platforms are all using reverse ratings. Not only do you rate the driver of your ride, but also the driver rates you back. When your rating on Uber falls below a 4.0, you may start being declined for future rides.

The most extreme example of how ratings data will be used in the future, however, comes from China. For the past few years the country has been experimenting with a program called the Social Credit System (SCS) which offers "social credit" rankings to citizens based on their behavior. In this system, you can be rewarded for doing voluntary military service or paying bills on time and punished for activities such as driving badly or posting fake news online.

Punishments can range from being denied passage on planes or trains to limiting your job prospects, while a good social credit score could mean more favorable interest rates or faster Visa approvals for travel. For many observers, the entire system seems like the ultimate science fiction dystopia scenario, where people can be ostracized merely for having a bad rating from a state-controlled system. Others suggest that these critiques are based on "worst-case scenarios far off in the future" and that the fears may be overblown.

In the future, these are exactly the sorts of questions that this megatrend of *Data Abundance* will raise. The more information we collect, the more challenges we will face about how to interpret it — and what implications those interpretations will have for our daily lives.

Thanks to social media and smart devices, companies and consumers are awash with data that they struggle to make sense of. The problem, in many cases, is that this data sets are compromised or too vast to extract meaningful insights. To cope with this problem, the groups that own and need to analyze the data will increasingly turn to machine learning to sift through the data and offer automated suggestions for key insights or actions to take.

Perhaps the most significant implication of this *Data Abundance* is around ownership and expectation. As consumers become huge producers of data through smart, connected, and personal devices, they will demand more control and ownership over the data they generate. They will become more savvy about how to use their information, more careful about whom they share with, and more demanding of what incentives they expect in order to share it willingly.

HOW TO USE DATA ABUNDANCE

BE WORTHY OF A CUSTOMER'S DATA.

The more control users demand over their data that is being collected from their actions, the more incentives organizations will have to offer for users to willingly share this data. These empowered customers will sometimes turn to extreme measures to reclaim ownership over their own data, from demanding policy changes to deleting their accounts altogether. The organizations that wish to continue to monetize the consumer data they hold will need to adjust to this new reality by offering more transparency, guaranteeing they will use consumer data in ethical ways and clearly demonstrating value back to their consumers.

ASK BETTER QUESTIONS FROM YOUR DATA.

In many cases, the issues that come from blindly following data or feeling overloaded by data start with a failure to ask the right questions of the data. Rather than filling cells in a spreadsheet, consider developing a data *strategy* to uncover what questions you would derive value from answering and then be thoughtful about how your existing data (or new data you would collect) could be used to answer these bigger and better questions.

CLEAN UP YOUR DATA.

Stop prioritizing quantity over quality in your data collection efforts. As you develop a better understanding of what makes good versus bad data for your company, take steps to purge polluted data from your existing databases and to update your systems to prevent unreliable information from entering your database in the first place.

THE EVOLUTION OF DATA ABUNDANCE

A review of past trends that relate to this Megatrend:

MEASURING LIFE (2012)
Tracking tools offer individualized data to
monitor and measure all areas of your life.

↓

OVERQUANTIFIED LIFE (2014)
Wearables offer new ways to collect data, yet
their usefulness remains limited to superficial
analysis that fails to offer actionable insights.

↓

PRIVACY PARANOIA (2014)
Data breaches lead to a new global paranoia about
what governments and brands know about us and how
they might use this information in illicit ways.

↓

SMALL DATA (2015)
As consumers increasingly collect their own information, brand-owned "big data"
become less valuable than immediately actionable "small data" owned by
consumers themselves.

↓

DATA OVERFLOW (2016)
An overload of personal, open, and corporate data leads organizations to go
beyond algorithms and look to artificial intelligence, curation, and startups to
make the data meaningful.

↓

DATA POLLUTION (2018)
As we create more methods for quantifying the world around us, data gets
manipulated, contaminated and sabotaged, making it harder to separate true
insights from useless noise.

DATA ABUNDANCE

12 PROTECTIVE TECH

WHAT'S THE MEGATREND?

As we increasingly rely on predictive technology that keeps us and our world safe and makes life more convenient, we must contend with the privacy trade-offs required to make it work.

DURING THE PAST DECADE, we have become accustomed to technology protecting us — whether we are aware of it or not — as we go about our business and daily life. On the way to the airport, we might receive a text message telling us that our flight's departure time has changed. When we make an unusually large purchase at a store, our bank might call or text to confirm that we actually made the transaction. After we sit at our desk for more than two hours, our wearable fitness tracker might vibrate to remind us to move around. When we get email, algorithms have already removed any suspected spam before it ever hits our inbox.

Smart, predictive technology not only helps us lead healthier, easier, safer and more productive lives; it also helps protect the environment and enjoy a more efficient society. However, the more we get used to these devices, the more blindly we rely on them, which has opened up all sorts of questions — from whether it's a good idea to let technology make certain decisions for us to whether we are leaving ourselves and our democratic process vulnerable to hackers, fraudsters, manipulators and others who might wish us harm. That's the heart of the *Protective Tech* megatrend, which promises to spark debate for many years about the double-edged trade-offs we must make to benefit from predictive technology.

To understand what's at stake, there is perhaps no better place to start than health care, where striking the right balance between convenience and privacy can have life-or-death consequences.

ROBOTHERAPY AND INSIDEABLES

Would you consider using a robot as your therapist? Dr. Alison Darcy thinks you should. She believes that people are more honest about themselves and their health when speaking with robots rather than humans. Robots, after all, can't judge us. A clinical research psychologist at the Stanford School of Medicine, Darcy developed an AI chatbot "therapist" known affectionately as Woebot. The tool is programmed to interact with patients just as cognitive behavioral therapists do: by asking open-ended questions and encouraging their clients to reflect on their emotions. The app-based chat tool is available on demand 24 hours a day and relies on common prompts such as, "How are you feeling?" to encourage people to be more forthcoming about their emotions.

Woebot is just one of many examples of AI-enabled tech being developed to help us better manage our mental health. Some of this predictive technology has live-saving potential. Facebook has been building tools that can detect content indicating that individuals might be considering harming themselves or others. The goal is for these tools to provide early warning signs to friends and family members so they can intervene quickly.

In 2013, researchers at the University of Brescia in Italy found that online gamblers who lost big tended to bet in a predictable sawtooth pattern. A team led by Harvard Medical School psychiatrist Howard Shaffer partnered with online gambling sites to use their data develop data-based algorithms that can intervene when someone engages in behavior that might indicate they could become a problem gambler.

Although the use of predictive technology to protect mental health is fairly new, smart technology has been helping us keep track of our bodies and how they are doing for a while. Wearable health trackers have experienced explosive growth as we use them to monitor our vital signs, including heart rate, sleep patterns, and even posture. A new wave of devices is even taking self-monitoring to the next level by working from inside our bodies. Often called "inside-ables," these microscopic devices, which are swallowed, injected, or implanted, send biometric information via electronic signals to help diagnose problems and track overall health.

PREDICTIVE HEALTHCARE

As the technology advances, these types of sensors will become cheaper to and easier to use, and therefore more commonplace. They'll go beyond identifying problems and begin to aid treatment by monitoring our health, tracking whether we take our medications, and even identify diseases before we are aware of any symptoms.

Health-tech startup FacePrint, for example, created a tool that can diagnose Parkinson's disease through using facial recognition software and was inspired by a high-school student's obsession with the work of psychologist Paul Ekman who studied "micro-expressions."

This is the future of healthcare, where everything from your facial expression in a selfie to the data streams from a fitness tracker can be used to proactively improve your health, diagnose your ailments and even predict suicide and intervene before it happens.

As tracking devices and predictive tech are used to manage our physical and mental health, the information these devices collect is also starting to be used in ways that make us uncomfortable.

For example, Rhea Vendors, a maker of automated retail machines, released a vending machine that can use facial recognition to refuse to sell certain unhealthy snacks to people based on their age, medical history, or past purchases. This "food-shaming," candy-denying vending machine is an example of many critics' worst fears about how personal health data might be misused in overreaching ways.

The tension between the desire for smart tech to help us manage our lives — in this case, our health — and our worry that it might infringe on privacy will only grow as this tech becomes more ubiquitous. It raises a natural question: Should we cede so many health and life decisions to machines?

Our homes and all the smart technology in them suggest that, at least in some environments, perhaps we already have.

AUTOMATED ADULTING

Imagine you are staying at a hotel and realize you forgot your toothbrush. You call down to reception to ask for one, and a few minutes later, a robotic butler brings it to your room. That's what you can expect at more than a dozen hotels working with a San Francisco Bay Area–based robotics start-up, Savioke. Savioke is a pioneer in the fast-emerging utilitarian world of service bots, small, robotic helpers adept at handling domestic tasks as quietly and efficiently as possible. Today you can buy robotic lawn mowers and intelligent ovens, which use cameras to "read" your food and determine how long to cook it. You can buy dirt-sensing vacuum cleaners, smart toilets and person-detecting door locks that anticipate when you are nearing the door or leaving the house.

Consider the many other tech-enabled tools that help us manage our domestic sphere, such as grocery shopping apps that remember our past orders, automatic texts that confirm our prescription refills, and personal finance apps that pay our bills. It's clear that "adulting" — taking care of all the mundane chores that responsible adults handle daily — is increasingly automated, a trend we first wrote about in 2016 and called Automated Adulthood. In the modern home, we don't have to remember to dust, clean, lock the doors, turn off the lights or even remember to flush the toilet: everything is done for us.

The same might soon apply to our workspaces. The Amsterdam headquarters of consulting firm Deloitte (known as the Edge) was described in 2015 as the "smartest building in the world." The building syncs with your phone and knows when you drive into the parking garage, suggests a desk for you based on the temperature you like to work in, and features an open atrium design with slight heat variations and air currents to make the inside space feel like the outdoors — even when it is raining outside.

As the *Protective Tech* megatrend plays out over the coming decade, a generation of young consumers will expect technology to optimize every waking moment of their lives. But as they become dependent on technology to take care of the mundane tasks of adulting, will they also lose the ability to handle more nuanced parts of having human relationships and turn to technology for those as well?

One example is the rightfully ridiculed BroApp, designed to help men "outsource" their relationships by automating texts reminding their girlfriends how much they love them and delivering other romantic messages. Less extreme versions of relationship management apps have popped up that help remember a partner's birthday or send automated greetings. Even the IFTTT (If This Then That) app, which allows users to create "recipes" for a sequence of actions across multiple apps, has a solution for hapless partners of the social media addicted: "Get a notification when your girlfriend posts a new picture so that you can like it before she gets mad."

There's no doubt the rise of predictive tech will continue to make our daily lives easier and safer even as we perhaps become too reliant on it for doing things we might be better off doing ourselves. However, the impact of smart technology on our environment has even more significant repercussions.

ANTI-POACHING DRONES AND AERIAL SURVEILLANCE

In 2019 I was lucky to join a team of South African scientists and rangers headed deep into the bush on a mission to help save rhinos. Our task that morning was chasing and tagging a black rhino by notching it — removing a small portion of skin from its ear. For decades, notching has been the primary method for tracking these endangered animals and protecting them from poachers. Now those teams on the ground are getting some help from the skies as well. Across Africa, conservation groups are using drones to police the wilderness, find and arrest poachers before they strike. They are among the many organizations turning to smart devices to automate the task of overseeing the land and protecting animals and the environment.

High above the Yangtze River Basin, the Chinese government is deploying a different kind of technology to impact the environment. The effort, known as the Tianhe (Sky River) Project, involves installing machines that produce silver iodide particles, which artificially induce the formation of clouds and rain. Early estimates suggest that this cloud-seeding process for manipulating the weather eventually could generate as much as 7 percent of China's overall annual water consumption, a huge boon for the country's 1.4 billion people.

Cloud seeding isn't always used for noble purposes. For example, in 2008 during the Summer Olympics, China used the technology to make sure that the clouds headed toward Beijing released their rain before getting to the capital. On a more personal level, one European company offers a high-end service targeted to anxious brides that uses that same cloud-seeding technology to dissipate clouds and prevent rain on their wedding day. The service starts at £100,000.

Together these cases raise complicated questions.

Certainly the world might benefit from a rainless Olympics, but is it ethical for a private company or even a government to alter the weather for the benefit of a single person or event? While drones can be used to protect endangered wildlife, what if they are used by paparazzi to capture illicit photos or by terrorists to disrupt air traffic control.

Alongside the benefit these technologies offer our world, there is often a corresponding cost to privacy and civil liberties.

Questions such as these are casting a long shadow on the *Protective Tech* megatrend. Watchdog groups and concerned citizens alike openly wonder at the true cost of all this protective technology and worry that it makes us vulnerable to opportunistic villains. We are already starting to see some of these villains emerge.

WHAT WE CAN LEARN FROM ESTONIA

Estonia, a former Soviet state along the Baltic Sea, is a nation of just 1.3 million people, but although it is geographically tiny, its technological sophistication is not. The first country in the world to declare access to the internet a basic human right, Estonia has become a case study of how a nation can abandon old systems and run many services online, from banking and taxes to voting.

Estonians are pioneers of digital identifiers, which are unique sets of digits assigned to every citizen, similar to a Social Security number in the United States. Because most significant tasks are done online and tracked with the digital identifier, many cumbersome processes that typically involve long hours completing paperwork — such as filing taxes, opening a bank account, or filing for a business license — are mostly automated.

HOW HACKERS MIGHT SAVE THE WORLD

As more countries digitally transform their governments and rely on smart technology to run them, they also become more attractive targets for cyberattacks. After recovering from several coordinated assaults in 2007, Estonia built tools to prevent them in the future. The country's approach to protecting its 2019 election from tampering has become an example of how to protect the integrity of the democratic election process.

Keeping tech-enabled election processes safe from bad actors who want to influence the results has become a top priority for most governments around the world, and they are getting help from an unexpected group. A few years ago, a collective of Hamburg-based hackers known as the Chaos Computer Club intentionally exposed security flaws in voting software ahead of an election in Germany. They were widely credited with protecting the integrity of the election process from potential Russian hackers. Today governments recruit these so-called white hat hackers who choose to use their skills for good, challenging them to hack into existing systems and paying them bounties if they succeed. By hacking an election system, they expose its vulnerabilities to be fixed before the criminally minded exploit it.

This approach to safeguarding tech-enabled election systems is receiving the support of big tech as well. Microsoft recently announced a free open-source election software, ElectionGuard, that promises to help governments better discover and prevent electoral hacking attempts.

While many countries would like to follow Estonia's example and digitally transform and protect their government systems, most find the prospect daunting. Estonia, after all, is a small country. For larger countries, abandoning behemoth analog systems seems nearly impossible. That's where private companies are stepping in, making previously challenging aspects of dealing with complex, bureaucratic legal and financial systems both easier and safer for consumers.

ONE-BUTTON LAWSUITS AND ROBOADVISORS

In 2015, Joshua Browder, an 18-year-old British American student, wrote software to automatically appeal dozens of parking tickets. In the next four years, his DoNotPay app helped people save more than $25 million and earned him a venture capital–funded deal of nearly $5 million to develop the platform further.

Since then, the app has expanded functionality and relaunched as "the world's first robot lawyer," promising to help people "fight corporations, beat bureaucracy, and sue anyone at the press of a button." It is being used for everything from helping people apply for housing when facing eviction to simplifying the process for consumers to sue large corporations after data breaches. The newest feature is a tool that lets users generate a free virtual credit card number to use when signing up for free trials of any service without using their real name. When the trial ends, the card declines to be charged and the free trial is over, without the need for the user to remember to cancel it.

The message this app and other digital tools that promise to proactively protect consumers send is clear: automation can be a guardian against predatory services and help consumers stand up for themselves.

Predictive technology will continue to augment the services that professionals provide, protecting consumers from paying exorbitant fees or receiving biased advice. But the same automated technology will lead to a growing tension between the professionals who keep up with tech advances and thus make themselves even more indispensable and those who resist its growing role until the moment they become obsolete.

PROTECTIVE TECH AT A GLANCE

In the future, lights will anticipate our arrival and turn themselves on. Health-tracking devices will silently monitor our vital signs, alerting us when something goes awry. AI-enabled investment trackers will manage our finances, making adjustments as necessary. Drones will protect our wilderness and police our skies. Digitized governments will allow us to file taxes accurately in minutes.

Predictive smart technology already makes our lives more convenient and safer. But in order to provide real-time utility, these technologies have to "listen," collecting information about us and our environment 24/7. As protective tech becomes more sophisticated, it will lead to more debates about how much of our daily lives should be trackable and how important personal privacy and individual liberties are when weighed against the broader interests of society.

HOW TO USE PROTECTIVE TECH

 BE A ROLE MODEL FOR TECHNOLOGY.
Much as children get their first impressions on how to act from their parents, robots are imprinted with their abilities from humans. For example, an early AI chatbot launched to learn how to engage in "casual and playful conversation" on Twitter famously devolved into a "racist asshole" within weeks. As learning technology gets smarter, it's evolution will largely come from watching humans and parsing the media that humans create— which leads to an unusual challenge for humanity. Just as we must serve as role models for our children, increasingly we will need to serve that same role for our technology as well.

 RECOGNIZE AND APPRECIATE THE PROTECTION.
Many of the ways that technology protects us can become so well hidden that we forget to even acknowledge, appreciate or value them. In the future, we will need to work harder to remain conscious of where technology offers this protection so we can avoid blind overreliance on it.

 DEMAND MORE TECHNOLOGY TRANSPARENCY.
The more potential applications we see for *Protective Tech*, the more important transparency will become in terms of who has access to provide it on our behalf. The positive or negative benefits to society will increasingly depend on the mission and ethics of those who have earned (or demand) the right to access it.

THE EVOLUTION OF PROTECTIVE TECH

A review of past trends that relate to this Megatrend:

PREDICTIVE PROTECTION (2015 + 2018)

Brands are increasingly creating smarter products that monitor our safety and health, alerting us when we need to take action.

⬇

AUTOMATED ADULTHOOD (2016)

As it is taking longer to emerge into full adulthood, innovative services are helping us automate common adult tasks.

⬇

ROBOT RENAISSANCE (2017 + 2019)

Advances in robotics, including human-like interfaces, are leading us to raise questions about how we relate to that technology.

⬇

INVISIBLE TECHNOLOGY (2017)

Technology becomes better at anticipating and predicting what we need while simultaneously blending more seamlessly and unnoticeably into our lives and the world around us.

⬇

PROTECTIVE TECH

13 FLUX COMMERCE

WHAT'S THE MEGATREND?

As the lines between industries erode, how we sell and buy anything changes constantly, leading to a continual disruption of business models, distribution channels, consumer expectations and even innovation itself.

IN 2012 THE SPANISH GOVERNMENT passed a devastating new tax. In a bid to institute economic reforms and austerity measures, the new legislation effectively increased the tax for theatrical shows from 8 percent to 21 percent. Over the next year, attendance in theaters across the country plummeted 30 percent.

Desperate theater owners tried all sorts of novel solutions to survive. One theater, for example, sold high-priced carrots — which were not taxed — for 16 euros and bundled them with "free" movie tickets. But perhaps the most creative solution came from the comedy theatre company Teatreneu. Entrance to their shows became free. But upon exiting, you paid a fee based on *exactly* how funny the performance was for you. Every seat was outfitted with a tablet that used facial tracking technology to detect every time you smiled. Each smile cost 30 euro cents, up to a maximum ticket price of 24 Euros. The pay-per-laugh initiative was an instant hit, generating a 35 percent spike in attendance and inspiring other comedy clubs to imitate Teatreneu's approach.

Around the same time Teatreneu was reinventing the way people paid to see a comedy show, a company called Casper was changing the way people were buying mattresses. Casper sells foam mattresses online and ships them, rolled and compressed, in a box approximately the size of a kitchen cabinet. A decade ago, the idea that people would buy a mattress without trying it first might have been unthinkable. Today, consumers are used to buying all sorts of things online without seeing them first — from shoes to prescription eyeglasses.

On the other side of the world, a former Japanese bookstore clerk named Yoshiyuki Morioka launched a bold experiment in the upmarket shopping district of Ginza in Tokyo. His Morioka Shoten bookstore captured the attention of the world for its radical business model: it only sold one book title at a time, devoting an entire week to author events and community discussions and engagement around that book.

On the surface, charging theater-goers by how much they smile, selling mattresses online, and launching a single-book bookstore may seem unrelated. Yet over the past decade, one of the most wide-ranging trends we have been tracking is the disruption not in what we choose to buy or who is selling it, but *how* those products and experiences are bought and sold. This megatrend, *Flux Commerce*, describes how successful companies are increasingly evolving their business models and distribution methods — aspects of the business that were once fixed — and changing how they innovate to keep up.

This is a topic that we have been tracking for years. Back in 2015 we introduced a trend that we called *Disruptive Distribution* — a term to describe how the way that products and services were being delivered to end consumers was dramatically shifting.

Perhaps nothing quite illustrates how companies are embracing *Flux Commerce* more than the growing number of companies boldly stepping outside their comfort zone to innovate and expand beyond their traditional industry boundaries.

THE INDUSTRY BLUR

There was a time when Red Bull was just an energy drink. Since the early nineties, the Austria-based brand has expanded into a growing media empire that includes live events, print publications, and even a 24/7 curated streaming television channel. This isn't the first time that Red Bull crossed industries in its line extension. The company has also acquired 15 sports teams across 11 sports including soccer, Formula 1 racing, sailing, surfing, ice hockey, and skateboarding. Why take the bold move across to other industries?

"As a major content provider, it is our goal to communicate and distribute the 'World of Red Bull' in all major media segments, from TV to print to new media to our music record label," Dietrich Mateschitz, Red Bull cofounder explains. "The total editorial media value plus the media assets created around the [sports] teams are superior to pure advertising expenditures."

Red Bull is one of many examples of how companies are willing to step outside the traditional boundaries of their industries to differentiate themselves from the competition and diversify to benefit from multiple revenue streams and capture more of their consumer's attention in the process.

Capital One, for example, has been transforming bank branches into comfortable cafes and co-working spaces. Retail brands such as West Elm, Muji, Taco Bell and Armani are all opening their own branded hotels, betting that customers who spend a night immersed with their products might buy more of them.

In the world of consulting, longtime players like IBM, Accenture, PwC and Deloitte are hoping to make inroads into the marketing industry with their new interactive and creative services groups. Powerful media brands like *The New York Times, Wall Street Journal, Forbes, and New York Magazine* have recently launched their own custom content studios where journalists work on the side to produce high quality content for brands.

Even Amazon has branched out beyond its online retail focus into the grocery market with the acquisition of Whole Foods and the launch of several grocery stores.

In the past, the lines between vertical industries were drawn clearly and definitively. Today not only are those lines shifting, but we are starting to question one of the most fundamental principles of business itself: ownership.

FROM OWNERSHIP TO USERSHIP

For decades, buying a car was a rite of passage — a symbol of freedom, responsibility, and adulthood. But the combination of older demographics moving into urban areas and the easy availability of ride-sharing services is leading many analysts to predict a widespread drop-off in the number of people who will want to own a car in the future.

It seems like, increasingly, we want *less* commitment for the things we pay for: We don't want to own a car — maintain it, park it, or wash it. We just want to *get* somewhere. So why pay for the high, upfront costs of owning a car when we can just pay for a ride? Similarly, why own an expensive cozy vacation home when we can pay to stay at someone else's home via Airbnb whenever we want?

This shift has led some economists to use the term "usership" rather than ownership to describe the kind of control we increasingly want over the products and services we need or want. In other words, we want to *use* a product, not necessarily *own* it. Consumers are interested in flexibility, not in long term commitment and fixed costs. And they are willing to pay for only the portion they use directly from its owner either on a case-by-case basis — such as taking an Uber or renting an Airbnb — or a recurrent one.

To respond to this shift from ownership to usership, companies across all industries have been transforming their businesses from a traditional up-front revenue model — in which they sell a product or service in exchange for a one-time fee — to subscription models. We've been writing extensively about this trend, which we dubbed *Subscription Commerce* back in 2014, and it shows no signs of slowing down.

Today, software such as Microsoft Office and Adobe's Creative Cloud, for example, are only offered for sale on a subscription basis. Movie theater chains are starting to offer a monthly unlimited movie subscription. Automakers like BMW and Volvo are experimenting with monthly subscription models that lets customers change cars every few months — or even more frequently. In the legal profession, longtime advice provider LegalZoom has been joined in recent years by more niche firms like Wevorce (a service that helps people file and handle their divorce). For a monthly fee, they offer customers access to lawyers, mediators, and legal resources whenever they need them.

Businesses have also adapted to the rise of usership by embracing shared marketplaces and even shared labor, a trend we also wrote about in 2014 and that we called the *Collaborative Economy*. In the hospitality industry, a service called Pared connects restaurants with temporary kitchen staff. Uber announced plans to start an on-demand staffing business called Uber Works. CargoX matches businesses in Brazil that need transportation with truckers whose rigs have extra space. Similarly, a platform called Flexe allows anyone to book remnant warehouse space when they need it. And the startup Spacious has launched an app that helps upscale New York restaurants offer their space during the day to people looking for coworking office space.

Although the rise of usership is driving the transformation of previously fixed business models to subscription and collaborative ones, it doesn't mean that we have abandoned "ownership" entirely. We are, after all, a fairly materialistic society. But where and how we buy products we wish to own is radically changing the retail industry.

RETAIL FLUX

Perhaps no industry has had to adapt to the constant changes of how we buy and sell more than retail. Dramatic shifts in how we buy just about everything along with growing consumer expectations have driven some retail analysts year after year to proclaim that this, in fact, will be the year of the "retail apocalypse." Of course, that doomsday prediction hasn't yet come true, but over the past decade, retails store environments have been changing to become more immersive, personalized, and dynamic.

In many retail fashion stores, for example, brands are using technologies such as smart mirrors that allow customers to compare outfits side by side, snap photos of themselves, or even call a store employee for assistance getting a new size or item. Brands are also investing in "nearables — location-based beacons that deliver discount offers or assistance to customers via mobile device or roaming sales associates. Similarly, home improvement stores like Lowe's and IKEA are using virtual or augmented reality to offer customers a way to visualize what a remodeling project will look like in their homes.

Major retailers are also experimenting with "robocarts" that guide customers through a store, syncing with their shopping lists to optimize their route and ensure they don't forget anything. Some are even transforming their spaces into cashier-free stores where customers scan a single code that identifies them and everything they've purchased, automatically charging them.

Retailers are also changing how they price their products, as well as how often and quickly that price is updated. "Surge pricing"—increasing the price of a product or service when demand for it is high—dynamically changes the retail price for everything from groceries to ride-sharing rides. In this world of instant price updates, some worry that in the future, some retailers will even deploy "price bots" that skillfully collude against customers to ensure we pay an algorithmically-maximized price at all times.

Significant changes to how we buy has not only dramatically shifted the strategies and approaches retailers use to sell products and services—it has also transformed how companies innovate them.

INNOVATING INNOVATION

Every day we are confronted with news stories about the wonderous benefits of the latest health craze. Activated charcoal traps toxins and chemicals in the gut, preventing their absorption! Algae capsules boost your brainpower and prevent heart disease! Acacia fiber relieves pain and reduces fat!

Some of these claims may actually be true. Some certainly aren't. Unfortunately, we are given so much conflicting advice—especially by get-rich-quick online marketers and "advice" websites—that most of us end up completely confused and extremely skeptical. We respond by increasingly moving on from fads faster than ever before—a trend, *Fad Fatigue*, that we wrote about in our 2017 report.

The enthusiasm around a "fad" has always been intense and viral. But fad fatigue has had a tremendous effect on how we buy (or not buy) products. We are simply moving on to the next flavor of the month faster and faster. This has put companies under tremendous pressure to find new ways to innovate. They are trying to find the "next big thing" and fear that nothing less than a complete overhaul of their business will be necessary to assure their relevance and survival. It has led some of the more desperate to naively look to recreate exactly what they see more innovative competitors doing — a trend we described as *Innovation Envy* in 2019.

Some companies are responding to this challenge by hosting innovation competitions (like hackathons), launching platforms to connect startups with internal teams, or creating "innovation labs" within their companies. Ford Motor Company, for example, launched its Research and Innovation Center, a lab in Silicon Valley focused on the intersection of cutting-edge technology and the driving experience. Open Innovation, Kraft Heinz Springboard, Adidas Brooklyn Creator Farm and countless other labs launched in the past several years. The examples were so plentiful that it led us in 2016 to describe a trend we called *Insourced Incubation* — to describe how companies were focused on bringing outside thinking into the organization.

Nordstrom, the high-end retailer, was one of the earliest to launch an innovation lab back in 2013. Two years later, the brand announced that it was shrinking its lab and reassigning its employees into other groups. When asked about it by online site Geekwire, a Nordstrom spokesperson said, "rather than just a team focused on innovation, it's now everyone's job." The natural evolution of any external skillset that starts with being "insourced" is to eventually become integrated into the overall way business is done.

Change is the new normal in business today. Companies are realizing that to continuously innovate the new business models, distribution methods, customer engagement tactics and more that they need to keep up with all this change — they must first innovate how they innovate.

How we buy and sell products, how much we are willing to pay for them, and whether we choose to own or rent them is changing drastically — and fast.

As the lines once distinctly drawn between industries erode almost completely, and as business models shift from products being sold not as products but as a service or subscription, and as distribution methods are transformed to eliminate middlemen, winners in this new economy are increasingly those who embrace the fast-changing and increasingly blurred nature of commerce — those who welcome the "flux" and move with it.

1. FIND THE BLUR.

As you think about how to transform your business strategy, consider what would happen if you put two unlikely models together. What if you sold cars the way that a donut shop sells donuts? Or what if Airbnb decided to start a pharmacy? These sorts of mind-bending questions encourage us to think outside our comfort zone and find new ideas in the "blur" between industries. Some of these ideas may seem farfetched and impossible, but they can lead to an actionable idea as you work your way backwards from crazy to possible.

2. BE STRATEGIC, NOT REACTIVE.

Often, companies will mistake invention for innovation. They are not the same thing. This common mistake can lead to shallow ideation, one-dimensional product or service ideas, and undifferentiated engagement with your customers. Look beyond products to consider new business models that integrate greater purpose and deliver more robust experiences that delight customers.

3. SEEK OUT AND SUPPORT THE INNOVATORS.

Nearly every successful corporate effort dedicated to innovation finds new ways to bring in entrepreneurs as a first step. Sometimes this takes the shape of startup competitions or newer tactics like the "switch pitch," where established brands pitch to startups the business challenges they face, then the startups partner with the brand to develop solutions. But besides looking outside for innovation, first look *inside* your company. Find the employees who are devoted to innovation — and who are often overlooked. Look for pockets of innovation within your own organization — teams that may already be doing interesting things — and support their initiatives and use them as a starting point.

THE EVOLUTION OF FLUX COMMERCE

A review of past trends that relate to this Megatrend:

HYPER-LOCAL COMMERCE (2013)

New services and technology make it easier for anyone to
invest in local businesses and buy from local merchants.

↓

INSTANT ENTREPRENEURS (2014)

As the barriers to starting a new business begin to fall, incentives and
tools mean anyone with an idea can launch a startup knowing
that the costs and risks of failure are not as high as before.

↓

COLLABORATIVE ECONOMY (2014)

New business models and tools allow consumers and brands to tap
the power of sharing and collaborating to find new ways to
buy, sell, and consume products and services.

↓

SUBSCRIPTION COMMERCE (2014)

More businesses and retailers use subscriptions to sell recurring services
or products to customers instead of focusing on one- time sales.

↓

DISRUPTIVE DISTRIBUTION (2015 + 2018)

Creators and makers use new models for distribution to disrupt the usual channels,
cut out middlemen, and build more direct connections with fans and buyers.

↓

REVERSE RETAIL (2015)

Brands increasingly invest in high touch in- store experiences to build
brand affinity and educate customers, while seamlessly integrating
online channels to complete actual purchases and fulfill orders.

↓

INSOURCED INCUBATION (2016)

Companies desperate to be more innovative increasingly look to bring
more outside innovators in- house, enticing them with funding,
beautiful co- working lab spaces, and a feel good pitch.

↓

continued ➜

FAD FATIGUE (2019)
Consumers get weary of innovations claiming to be the
next big thing and assume none will last long.

INNOVATION ENVY (2019)
Fear leads entrepreneurs, businesses, and institutions to envy
competitors and approach innovation with admiration or desperation.

FLUX COMMERCE

PART III
Previous Trend Reports
(2011–2019)

OVERVIEW:

How to Read These Past Trend Reports

"The events of the past can be made to prove anything
if they are arranged in a suitable pattern."

—A. J. P. TAYLOR, Historian

IMAGINE FOR A MOMENT that you could go back in time and relive a moment from your life ten years ago. What might you think as you look back on how you used to see the world and what you once believed? Perhaps you have changed dramatically, or perhaps you're largely the same. Either way, most of us rarely get this sort of keyhole glimpse to witness our own growth.

The journey to write and update this book annually has given me a constant chance to do that. As I look back over the past ten years, I realize what a gift this is. I also have struggled with the temptation to engage in a bit of revisionist history.

Should I leave every word of every trend prediction unchanged from its original state? What would provide the most value for people reading these insights a decade or two or three later? The answer to both questions, I felt, was to update some trends for clarity, but not to change their meaning or intent.

The trends in this section tell a story about an evolving point of view of our culture. Each year I can honestly say—based solely on the feedback of readers — the trends have gotten more insightful and enduring. However, they haven't all been winners.

In the following pages, you will see a visual and detailed compilation of every past trend published since 2011. For each year, I will start with a retrospective to give you a sense of the highlights and themes from that report, followed by a letter grade rating of how every trend fared over the years.

The grades range from A to D. Aside from flipping through this section to see the D graded trends (which I know you will do simply out of curiosity), you might wonder why no trends received an F grade?

I believe an F should be reserved for a trend that was never accurate, a situation that doesn't really apply to these trends because at the time they were published they were indeed non-obvious.

Those that received a D just failed to last beyond the initial year they were predicted.

It is impossible to grade yourself, so these ratings are not based on my personal assessments. Instead, my team and I gathered feedback from thousands of professionals who have participated in or listened to one of my signature keynotes or one of our workshops around the world. We combined their feedback with insights from readers who wrote to us or commented on the research online.

In addition, I made it a habit within our team to consistently seek out new examples of previously predicted trends so we could build a library and see just how many more relevant examples would come up since a trend was originally published.

This annual ritual of reviewing, grading, and critiquing past trends has made these predictions better. We learn from our mistakes as much as we celebrate our successes, and the book you hold in your hands today is the product of a decade of refinement.

As I shared early in this book, I think the most beautiful thing about well curated trends is that new ones don't replace old ones. Rather, they all present a collection of observations and insights that I hope will spur your thinking about opportunities today while reminding you that the best way to win the future is to become a student of the accelerating present.

Either way, the trends can be a spark for new ideas and an instigator for innovation. I hope this summary of past trends offers both of these things, as well as an interesting look back at the evolution of the last decade of research and insights.

BROWSE ALL PAST TRENDS AND DOWNLOAD EXCERPTS

www.nonobvious.com/trends

THE 2011 NON-OBVIOUS TRENDS OVERVIEW

Likeonomics
Approachable Celebrity
Desperate Simplification
Essential Integration
Rise of Curation
Visualized Data
App-fication of the Web
ReImagining Charity
Employees as Heroes
Locationcasting
Brutal Transparency
Addictive Randomness
Culting of Retail

THE 2012 NON-OBVIOUS TRENDS OVERVIEW

Corporate Humanism
Ethnomimicry
Social Loneliness
Pointillist Filmmaking
Measuring Life
Co-Curation
Charitable Engagement
Medici Marketing
Digital Afterlife
Real-Time Logistics
Social Artivism
Civic Engagement 2.0
Tagging Reality
Changesourcing
Retail Theater

THE 2013 NON-OBVIOUS TRENDS OVERVIEW

Optimistic Aging
Human Banking
Mefunding
Branded Inspiration
Backstorytelling

Healthy Content
Degree-Free Learning
Precious Print
Partnership Publishing
Microinnovation
Social Visualization
Heroic Design
Hyper Local Commerce
Powered by Women
Shoptimization

THE 2014 NON-OBVIOUS TRENDS OVERVIEW

Desperate Detox
Media Bingeing
Obsessive Productivity
Lovable Imperfection
Branded Utility
Shareable Humanity
Curated Sensationalism
Distributed Expertise
Anti-stereotyping
Privacy Paranoia
Overquantified Life
Microdesign
Subscription Commerce
Instant Entrepreneurs
Collaborative Economy

THE 2015 NON-OBVIOUS TRENDS OVERVIEW

Everyday Stardom
Selfie Confidence
Mainstream Mindfulness
Branded Benevolence
Reverse Retail
Reluctant Marketer
Glanceable Content
Mood Matching
Experimedia
Unperfection

Predictive Protection
Engineered Addiction
Small Data
Disruptive Distribution
Micro Consumption

THE 2016 NON-OBVIOUS TRENDS OVERVIEW

E-mpulse Buying
Strategic Downgrading
Optimistic Aging
B2Beyond Marketing
Personality Mapping
Branded Utility
Mainstream Multiculturalism
Earned Consumption
Anti-stereotyping
Virtual Empathy
Data Overflow
Heroic Design
Insourced Incubation
Automated Adulthood
Obsessive Productivity

THE 2017 NON-OBVIOUS TRENDS OVERVIEW

Fierce Femininity
Side Quirks
Desperate Detox
Passive Loyalty
Authentic Fameseekers
Lovable Unperfection
Preserved Past
Deep Diving
Precious Print
Invisible Technology
Robot Renaissance
Self-Aware Data
Moonshot Entrepreneurship
Outrageous Outsiders
Mainstream Mindfulness

THE 2018 NON-OBVIOUS TRENDS OVERVIEW

Truthing
Ungendered
Enlightened Consumption
Overtargeting
Brand Stand
Backstorytelling
Manipulated Outrage
Light-Speed Learning
Virtual Empathy
Human Mode
Data Pollution
Predictive Protection
Approachable Luxury
Touchworthy
Disruptive Distribution

THE 2019 NON-OBVIOUS TRENDS OVERVIEW

Strategic Spectacle
Muddled Masculinity
Side Quirks
Artificial Influence
Retrotrust
B2Beyond Marketing
Fad Fatigue
Extreme Uncluttering
Deliberate Downgrading
Enterprise Empathy
Innovation Envy
Robot Renaissance
Good Speed
Overwealthy
Passive Loyalty

THE 2011 NON-OBVIOUS TREND REPORT OVERVIEW

Originally published January 2, 2011
Original Format: Visual presentation

The Backstory + Retrospective

The first edition of the Non-Obvious Trend Report focused solely on marketing and social media trends. The report used a 20-page visual style and included a short description of the trend along with three or four stories to illustrate each one. Despite its limited scope, the report quickly went viral when it was released, being viewed more than 100,000 times in the first several weeks of publication alone.

Some of the most popular trends introduced many firsts. The report was one of the first to predict the *Rise of Curation,* a precursor to the explosion of content marketing, and *Instant PR & Customer Care,* the rapid growth of real-time customer service through social media. It also defined the related trends of *Brutal Transparency*, *Corporate Humanity,* and *Employees as Heroes,* which all demonstrated a deeper level of transparency and humanity in marketing campaigns.

The most popular trend from the first report was undoubtedly *Likeonomics,* the idea that people choose to do business with people they like. That popular concept inspired a book of the same title, which I wrote and published the following year.

2011 TRENDS AT A GLANCE

 Likeonomics

 Approachable Celebrity

 Desperate Simplification

 Essential Integration

 Rise of Curation

 Visualized Data

 Crowdsourced Innovation

 Instant PR & Customer Service

 App-fication of the Web

 ReImagining Charity

 Employees as Heroes

 Locationcasting

 Brutal Transparency

 Addictive Randomness

 Culting of Retail

LIKEONOMICS

Brands, products, and services succeed by being more human, mission driven, and personally likeable through their policies and people, gaining an advantage over less empathetic competitors.

Trend Longevity Rating A

The fundamental truth of human relationships underlying this trend keeps growing as more brands focus on building personal connections with customers and being consistently likeable.

APPROACHABLE CELEBRITY

As social media allow direct access to previously unreachable celebrities, politicians, and athletes, we see more of their personalities, for better or worse, and can engage with them as real people.

Trend Longevity Rating B

Using social media to directly engage famous people has become easy, but that ease has forced celebrities to find new ways to manage the volume, filter cyberstalkers, and make themselves less approachable.

DESPERATE SIMPLIFICATION

Information overload drives consumers to desperately seek simplicity, aiming for balance through activities such as defriending and finding basic products and sites to help simplify everything.

Trend Longevity Rating B

While "infobesity" persists, consumers' need for simplicity gives way to tools that focus on optimizing or curating instead of culling friendships or content. This trend continues but with less desperation.

ESSENTIAL INTEGRATION

Marketers' biggest problem continues to be integrating efforts, which can be hard with few good examples. Yet the biggest successes feature a new level of integration that is still rare in the marketing world.

Trend Longevity Rating B

During the past four years, integration becomes an even greater issue and daily struggle for marketers. With more tools and platforms to assist, this has become less of a trend and more of a standard practice.

RISE OF CURATION

Brands increasingly use curation as a much-needed filter to help find and bring together useful or entertaining content to win more trust and attention from consumers.

Trend Longevity Rating A

This trend successfully anticipated the explosion of content marketing and the importance for brands to focus on sharing expertise generously online with their consumers as a way to grow trust.

VISUALIZED DATA

To make sense of a real-time stream of information, more event managers, news organizations, and brands turn to visualization to leverage data, better understand it, and tell a clearer story.

Trend Longevity Rating B

The widespread overuse of infographics has created more skepticism of visualization, but better user interfaces, gamified design, and narrative storytelling continue to stand out and attract attention.

CROWDSOURCED INNOVATION

Brands turn to crowdsourced platforms to collect ideas from consumers in exchange for the reward of recognition, financial earning, and simply being heard by the brands they purchase from every day.

Trend Longevity Rating C+

The growth of platforms for idea generation to problem solving continue, but the original narrow brand-oriented focus of this trend failed to account for other types of marketplaces.

INSTANT PR & CUSTOMER SERVICE

Real-time contact becomes essential as communications teams focus on instant PR to manage social crises and augment customer service with methods to deal with problems in the here and now.

Trend Longevity Rating B

Customer service through social channels has grown dramatically, but today it is not solely driven by negative situations (as originally predicted) but rather used as a tool for positive engagement as well.

APP-FICATION OF THE WEB

As more innovative apps let consumers bypass the web for transactions and leisure, many activities from online banking to online shopping will shift to apps instead of the Internet.

Trend Longevity Rating D

Apps have grown dramatically, but the idea of doing everything through apps never happened. Instead, responsive design has made it more important to allow anyone to use any size screen on any device.

REIMAGINING CHARITY

Brands and entrepreneurs create innovative new models for social good, reinventing how people can do everything from donating money to sharing time and specific skills.

Trend Longevity Rating B

This trend reflected a dramatic growth in how nonprofits and charities used digital tools. While this has continued, the efforts are more commonplace and less of a "redefinition."

BRUTAL TRANSPARENCY

Aggressive honesty will lead to edgier and more effective marketing as brands reveal this unexpected tactic that consumers welcome.

Trend Longevity Rating A

The growth of social platforms and content marketing allows brands to share more truths about their business. While some may not be quite as "brutal," this honesty continues to build trust.

EMPLOYEES AS HEROES

Brands of all sizes aim to prove their humanity by emphasizing employees as the solvers of problems and creators of innovation. Such stories anchor the company's mission in the world.

Trend Longevity Rating B

This trend has expanded far beyond the tech firms initially featured as employees are increasingly valued in ads, showcased by brands with high loyalty, and seen as visible and important ambassadors for a brand.

ADDICTIVE RANDOMNESS

Brands increasingly will use the addictive power of random content to engage consumers. This will lead to more campaigns where consumers can add content to a central archive to browse.

Trend Longevity Rating D

While this idea might still be used selectively in campaigns, it is a good example of the sort of trend that we predicted early on that really should have been nothing more than an *ingredient* in a broader trend.

LOCATIONCASTING

More consumers choose to broadcast their locations, enabling brands to tailor messages to a specific site and create more opportunities to engage their customers in real life.

Trend Longevity Rating B

Mobile marketing increasingly offers geotargeting options. However consumers continue to be wary of privacy concerns and worry about the potential for "geospamming" as they walk down the street.

CULTING OF RETAIL

The best retailers create passionate users who not only buy products, but also rave about their experiences. They inspire their social networks to try for themselves.

Trend Longevity Rating A

The rise of social media enables a continued cult-like belief in brands and a willingness from fans to not only spend money on products and services, but also act as an ambassador for the brand.

THE 2012 NON-OBVIOUS TREND REPORT OVERVIEW

Originally published January 2, 2012
Original Format: Visual presentation

The Backstory + Retrospective

Capitalizing on the success of the first year's report, the second edition continued the focus on marketing and social media trends and surpassed the original's popularity. Topics covered in this edition included the sensitive yet emerging field of the *Digital Afterlife*, the rise of *Social Loneliness,* and the growth of *Corporate Humanism.* In contrast to the inaugural report, this update took a more human tone as many of the trends described cultural shifts and consumer behavior.

The second year had a few big hits as well as a few big misses. The overall trends that centered on the growth of humanity in companies and consumers stood the test of time. On the flip side, several trends from this year turned out to be overly quirky niche concepts. *Pointillist Filmmaking* and *Social Artivism* did not quantifiably take off as expected.

The mix of trends helped me hone the process and make a big leap the following year in both the quality of the predictions and the detail behind them.

CORPORATE HUMANISM

Companies find their humanity as they create more consumer-friendly policies and practices, spend more time listening to customers, and encourage employees to represent them in public.

Trend Longevity Rating

This may be the most enduring of all the trends we have predicted over the past nine years as we constantly see new examples of companies finding their humanity and avoiding facelessness.

ETHNOMIMICRY

Ethnographic analysis of how people interact in the real world inspires new social tools or products that mimic human behavior and social interaction as well as fit our lives.

Trend Longevity Rating

While some of the examples in this trend were dated (Google+), the concept of companies watching human interaction and tailoring products and services accordingly continues to have relevance.

SOCIAL LONELINESS

Despite online connections, people feel a real-world sense of loneliness, prompting them to seek ways to create deeper friendships or at least a chance to connect with people in deeper ways.

Trend Longevity Rating

Loneliness persists, and our digital connectivity continues to be a double-edged sword, making us feel more connected and isolated simultaneously, particularly among youth and the elderly.

POINTILLIST FILMMAKING

Named after the painting form using dots to create larger images, this trend describes a form of collaborative filmmaking in which numerous short clips are merged to tell a broader story through video.

Trend Longevity Rating D

This trend is perhaps my favorite disappointment. I loved the idea, but it was just too narrow to truly grow into a full trend and should have been an ingredient that elevated to a bigger idea.

CHARITABLE ENGAGEMENT

More charities rethink their focus on quick donations and instead promote participation through gaming and other methods of behavioral engagement.

Trend Longevity Rating B

While charities and nonprofits find more ways to engage donors , the predicted focus on participation hasn't really overtaken the breakdown between short-term fundraising and longer-term engagement.

MEASURING LIFE

A growing range of tracking tools handle individualized data to monitor and measure all areas of your life. They allow you to track your own health, measure your social influence, and set goals.

Trend Longevity Rating A

What was a big idea in 2012 has now become mainstream as we seem surrounded by tracking devices — so this trend undeniably accelerated.

MEDICI MARKETING

Inspired by the book *The Medici Effect*, this trend describes how thinking from multiple disciplines is combined to make marketing more engaging, creative, or useful.

Trend Longevity Rating B+

Though the book is still excellent, the name was too limiting to describe the scope of this trend — but the idea that marketing is (and should be) a melting pot for multidisciplinary thinking continues.

CO-CURATION

Curation gets more collaborative as amateurs and experts combine forces online to add their unique points of view and bring together multiple angles of many issues.

Trend Longevity Rating B+

Even as new tools have made it easier for anyone to curate information, the idea that this would lead to more collaboration around that curation was perhaps overly optimistic and hasn't come to fruition.

DIGITAL AFTERLIFE

During the past year, more companies started to focus on the digital afterlife, creating tools, education, and services to help manage all the data that loved ones leave behind when they die.

Trend Longevity Rating B

This trend perhaps more than any other exemplifies the frustrating reality of a trend that always seems to be emerging as a mainstream idea but never quite makes it into the wider conversation.

REAL-TIME LOGISTICS

Tech-savvy businesses use real-time conversation in social media to generate insights that help with supply chain and logistical planning to eliminate waste and maximize profits.

Trend Longevity Rating

Supply chain software continues to grow more sophisticated as large retailers and other distributors implement new tools to get better forecasts and leverage social conversation data to run better.

TAGGING REALITY

Better-quality mobile cameras allow developers to create tools that can tag any object in reality to unlock interactive content.

Trend Longevity Rating

The prevalent use of QR codes and tags that mapped reality to the online world seemed in 2012 as if it would be huge, but the trend never materialized as originally predicted.

SOCIAL ARTIVISM

The intersection between art and activism, known increasingly as *artivism*, get social as artists see social tools to reach more people and create greater societal impact.

Trend Longevity Rating

Art is used frequently for activism, and social media amplify it, but this trend should have been part of an elevated idea that went beyond just art for social issues.

CHANGESOURCING

Crowdsourcing itself is evolving beyond sharing information to a point where people can use the collaborative power of the crowd to achieve personal, social, or political change.

Trend Longevity Rating

The basic idea behind this trend focuses on crowdsourcing moving beyond information and into action as people tap the power of crowds to achieve real things, which continues today.

CIVIC ENGAGEMENT 2.0

A growing range of digital tools allows people to engage more actively with local governments on everything from reporting potholes to offering suggestions for improving their communities.

Trend Longevity Rating

Though civic engagement hasn't multiplied yearly, more people are adopting these tools to allow deeper citizen engagement, and tech-savvy cities are helping this trend accelerate into the mainstream.

RETAIL THEATER

In the coming year, more retail stores will create unique experiences using the principles of theater to engage customers with memorable experiences.

Trend Longevity Rating

Retailers have tried to get even more theatrical to combat the dangers of showrooms and the rise of online retail. If anything, this is making retail experiences even more interactive and dramatic than before.

THE 2013 NON-OBVIOUS TREND REPORT OVERVIEW

Originally published December 10, 2012
Original Format: Visual presentation + ebook

The Backstory + Retrospective

In the third year of the trend report, the level of detail expanded to more than 100 pages as the report featured more real-life examples and broader analysis. This edition of the Non-Obvious Trend Report did not originally use the five categories introduced later for alignment with future years, so I retroactively applied them and created the icons. This was also the first year that I produced a companion ebook, which was sold online and included tips on how to put the trends into action.

Thanks to the audience built from the first two editions, this was an instant No. 1 business best seller online. Trends that resonated most from this report included *Precious Print,* on the importance of physical printed objects; *Rise of Women,* on growth of female leaders in the workplace; *Backstorytelling, on* why people trust organizations that tell better stories; and *Shoptimization,* on the growing focus in retail experiences on making it easier and faster for customers to buy. Many of the ideas and themes introduced this year continued to resonate and affect later years of trend predictions. They even provided early inspiration for some megatrends introduced in this book.

2013 TRENDS AT A GLANCE

 Optimistic Aging

 Human Banking

 Mefunding

 Branded Inspiration

 Backstorytelling

 Healthy Content

 Degree-Free Learning

 Precious Print

 Partnership Publishing

 Microinnovation

 Social Visualization

 Heroic Design

 Hyper Local Commerce

 Powered by Women

 Shoptimization

OPTIMISTIC AGING

A wealth of online content and new social networks inspires people of all ages to feel more optimistic about getting older.

Trend Longevity Rating B

This sense of optimism about the future remains intact but is increasingly tempered by rising fears about the long-term security of the environment, divisive politics, and a global economy in flux.

HUMAN BANKING

Aiming to change years of growing distrust, banks finally uncover their human side by taking a more authentic approach to services and developing real relationships with customers.

Trend Longevity Rating B

Recurring financial crises and immoral activities underscore the importance of this trend, but growing inequality and continued distrust of banks remain hard to overcome.

MEFUNDING

Crowdfunding gets personal as individuals use it to seek financial support for everything from taking a life-changing trip to paying for college.

Trend Longevity Rating C

Although many sites featured as part of this trend remain available for donations, the widespread use of tools to raise personal funding has not accelerated the way we initially anticipated.

BRANDED INSPIRATION

Brands create awe-inspiring moments, innovative ideas, and dramatic stunts to capture attention and sometimes demonstrate their values to the world.

Trend Longevity Rating **B**

While this trend was about using big moments for inspiration, we continue to see a reliance on stunts to attract attention, an idea also reflected in our *Strategic Spectacle* trend from 2019.

DEGREE-FREE LEARNING

The quality of e-learning content explodes as more students consider alternatives to traditional college educations.

Trend Longevity Rating **B+**

Lifelong learners and those starting their careers continue to seek direct ways to learn new skills, solve problems, and get smarter without the necessity for a degree attached to that knowledge.

BACKSTORYTELLING

Organizations discover that taking people behind the scenes of their brand and history is one of the most powerful ways to inspire loyalty and drive purchase.

Trend Longevity Rating **A**

As earning trust continues to be a challenge, the impact of using stories to offer a reason to believe in a brand's mission and share it with others continues to be effective and necessary.

PRECIOUS PRINT

Thanks to our digital-everything culture, the few objects and moments we choose to interact with in print become more valuable.

Trend Longevity Rating **A**

The fact that we place even more value on the things that are printed because they are more valuable and rarer has continued unabated, leading us to bring this trend back in 2017.

HEALTHY CONTENT

Health care organizations feel pressure to create more useful and substantial health content to satisfy increasingly empowered patients who are skeptical of messages delivered in other ways.

Trend Longevity Rating **A**

The wealth of content about health online has exploded, as has the volume of credible and authoritative health care organizations publishing and sharing this content in multiple formats online.

PARTNERSHIP PUBLISHING

Aspiring authors, lacking a platform, and seasoned publishing professionals, in need of partners and content, team up to create a new "do-it-together" model of publishing.

Trend Longevity Rating **B**

This trend inspired my wife and I to start Ideapress Publishing in 2014 and still drives a shift in publishing but has led many entrants of questionable ethics and quality into the industry.

MICROINNOVATION

Thinking small becomes the new competitive advantage as slight changes to features or benefits create big value.

Trend Longevity Rating A-

The focus on making incremental changes to products in ways that can deliver ongoing value continues to drive many companies to innovate in small, sometimes hard-to-notice but still measurable ways.

HYPER LOCAL COMMERCE

New services and technology make it easier for anyone to invest in local businesses and buy from local merchants.

Trend Longevity Rating B

While local commerce continues to matter, threats from turnkey online competitors and the ability to have anything delivered make this a trend that has diminished in importance.

SOCIAL VISUALIZATION

To make data more accessible, new tools and technologies allow people to visualize content as part of their social profiles and online conversations.

Trend Longevity Rating A-

Tools for visualizing data continue to be commonplace and popular. This is one of those trends that were emerging when first written but seem obvious and still accurate.

POWERED BY WOMEN

Business leaders, pop culture, and ground-breaking new research inter-sect to prove that our ideal future will be led by strong and innovative women working on the front lines.

Trend Longevity Rating A

As women take increasingly prom-inent roles in business and culture, this trend remains a powerful force. It was the precursor to a popular 2017 trend, *Fierce Femininity*.

HEROIC DESIGN

Design takes a leading role in the invention and adoption of new prod-ucts, ideas, and campaigns to help change the world.

Trend Longevity Rating A

The growth of design thinking and a continued global need for audacious solutions to problems facing human-kind have made this a trend we see renewed examples of every year.

SHOPTIMIZATION

The proliferation of smart phones, new mobile apps, and startups lets consumers optimize and enhance the process of shopping for anything online and off.

Trend Longevity Rating A

Shopping experiences are optimized as retailers in all categories develop better mobile-enabled interfaces, smarter kiosks, easy-to-use apps, and a faster one-button checkout process.

THE 2014 NON-OBVIOUS TREND REPORT OVERVIEW

Originally published February 18, 2014
Original Format: Visual presentation + ebook

The Backstory + Retrospective

The fourth edition of the trend report was heavily influenced by a dramatic growth in my speaking appearances at conferences across the world. The demand and popularity of the report also led me to leave my role at Ogilvy after eight years to become an entrepreneur, start my own consulting business, and launch a publishing business.

For the first time, the trends were broken down into five categories: Culture + Consumer Behavior, Marketing + Social Media, Economics + Entrepreneurship, Technology + Design, and Media + Education. Some of the most popular trends from this year were *Desperate Detox,* about consumers hungry to escape the ever-present technology around them; *Curated Sensationalism,* on the increasing use of attention-grabbing headlines; *Subscription Commerce,* about long-established brands and products shifting to a subscription model; *Branded Utility,* on brands making their marketing more useful; and *Obsessive Productivity,* about people's desire to optimize their time in any way possible. These categories were used for the next five years.

This report also incorporated some of the trend research on health care that co-author Fard Johnmar and I published in our book *ePatient 2015.*

2014 TRENDS AT A GLANCE

 Desperate Detox

 Media Bingeing

 Obsessive Productivity

 Lovable Imperfection

 Branded Utility

 Shareable Humanity

 Curated Sensationalism

 Distributed Expertise

 Anti-stereotyping

 Privacy Paranoia

 Overquantified Life

 Microdesign

 Subscription Commerce

 Instant Entrepreneurs

 Collaborative Economy

DESPERATE DETOX

Consumers try to connect more authentically with others and seek out moments of reflection by intentionally disconnecting from the technology surrounding them.

Trend Longevity Rating

As technology remains omnipresent in our lives, we continue to see new examples of this trend in action almost every week. That led us to bring it back for our 2017 report.

MEDIA BINGEING

As more media and entertainment are available from any device on demand, consumers binge and are willing to pay extra for the convenience.

Trend Longevity Rating

As streaming options grow exponentially, we will see some fatigue with the idea of binge-watching as consumers feel overloaded and no longer obliged to stay up to date on every show.

OBSESSIVE PRODUCTIVITY

With thousands of life-optimizing apps and instant advice from social media-savvy self-help gurus, becoming more productive has become the ultimate obsession.

Trend Longevity Rating

People continue to fret over productivity as new books promise tips for life optimization. Many hack their daily chores and seek to save time through any means possible.

LOVABLE IMPERFECTION

Consumers search for true authenticity and reward minor imperfections in products, personalities, and brands by showing greater loyalty and trust.

Trend Longevity Rating A

In the nine years of this report, this trend has been among our most popular. We brought it back in the 2015 report as *Unperfection* and in 2018 as *Lovable Unperfection*. It remains one of our most popular trends.

CURATED SENSATIONALISM

As the line between news and entertainment blurs, smart curation displaces journalism as engaging content is paired with sensational headlines to drive millions of views.

Trend Longevity Rating A

Media continue to rely on sensationalism, which makes this trend a precursor to many other popular trends in later years, including *Truthing*, *Manipulated Outrage*, and *Strategic Spectacle*.

BRANDED UTILITY

Brands use content marketing and greater integration between marketing and operations centers to augment promotions with real ways to add value to customer's lives.

Trend Longevity Rating A

As content marketing continues to grow, brands increasingly find new ways to provide value, answer questions, and use marketing as a tool for education rather than purely for promotion.

DISTRIBUTED EXPERTISE

The idea of expertise itself shifts to become more inclusive, less academic, and more widely available on demand and in real time.

Trend Longevity Rating A-

Learning through experts online in many formats is gaining popularity, and learning platforms are growing quickly. Our ability to access expertise in real time will keep rising.

SHAREABLE HUMANITY

Content shared on social media gets more emotional as people share amazing examples of humanity and as brands inject more feelings into marketing communications efforts.

Trend Longevity Rating C

While human stories matter, this trend was negatively affected by fatigue from overly dramatic media stories and click-baiting headlines, which have made people far more skeptical of such stories.

ANTI-STEREOTYPING

Across media and entertainment, gender roles start to reverse, assumptions about alternative lifestyles are challenged, diversity increases, and perceptions of how people are defined continue to evolve.

Trend Longevity Rating A-

We see new stories that help us reevaluate people, see gender as fluid, and challenge our long-held assumptions about identity and blurring of what were once distinct lines.

PRIVACY PARANOIA

New data breaches are leading to a new global sense of paranoia about what governments and brands know about us and how they might use big data in potentially harmful ways.

Trend Longevity Rating **C**

While privacy persists as a concern, we are seeing this paranoia shift to empowerment as better oversight makes organizations misusing data far harder.

SUBSCRIPTION COMMERCE

More businesses and retailers use subscriptions to sell recurring services or products to customers instead of focusing on one-time sales.

Trend Longevity Rating **B–**

More industries and brands are turning to the lessons of subscription commerce, but it has led to burnout as consumers sometimes long for buying products or services the old way.

OVERQUANTIFIED LIFE

The value of personal data from wearable devices, for example, is obscured by cute infographics and superficial results that prevent thoughtful analysis of the data and effects on life decisions.

Trend Longevity Rating **B**

While finding value from the data we collect on ourselves continues to be a challenge, the analytical tools and personal desire to make such data actionable are helping manage the downside.

INSTANT ENTREPRENEURS

As the barriers to starting a new business begin to fall, incentives and tools mean anyone with an idea can launch a startup knowing that the costs and risks of failure are not as high as before.

Trend Longevity Rating **A**

While entrepreneurship appeals to more professionals, governments around the world continue to see it as a growth engine and work to make starting a business easier for anyone.

MICRODESIGN

As communication becomes more visual, design gains more respect, and demand for design skills grows, leading to easier access to bite-sized chunks of design expertise.

Trend Longevity Rating **B**

While the need for design expertise continues to grow, the narrow vision of this trend solely focused on design resources has limited application or relevance in wider situations.

COLLABORATIVE ECONOMY

New business models and tools allow consumers and brands to tap the power of sharing and collaborating to find new ways to buy, sell, and consume products and services.

Trend Longevity Rating **A**

We are firmly in the middle of the "sharing economy" as the idea of ownership shifts, people use and share products without owning them, and the economy stays collaborative.

THE 2015 NON-OBVIOUS TREND REPORT OVERVIEW

Originally published March 1, 2015
Original Format: Hardcover + Paperback + ebook

The Backstory + Retrospective

This year Non-Obvious was first published in hardcover format, and the trend report truly took off. The book was an instant Wall Street Journal best seller. For the first time it revealed my full process of trend curation, which I had shared previously only in private corporate workshops.

In addition to the explanations about becoming a trend curator and using my Haystack Method, the report introduced several popular trends that drew worldwide media attention. A few highlights from this report included *Unperfection,* about the preference people often have for naturally flawed and more human products and leaders; *Small Data,* on the personal information consumers collect on their own behavior; *Everyday Stardom,* about sometimes unrealistic consumer expectations that they are always VIPs; and *Selfie Confidence,* on the counterintuitive idea that taking and sharing selfies may be a form of building self-esteem.

Beyond the trends, the book's popularity this year introduced trend curation to a much broader audience, and the concept began to resonate globally. The book was contracted for six translated editions, and my speaking and workshop invitations, including more global appearances. The book's success also allowed the Non-Obvious Company to bring on more partners and team members, which in turn allowed us to expand the research and curation abilities and make the future reports even stronger.

2015 TRENDS AT A GLANCE

 Everyday Stardom

 Selfie Confidence

 Mainstream Mindfulness

 Branded Benevolence

 Reverse Retail

 Reluctant Marketer

 Glanceable Content

 Mood Matching

 Experimedia

 Unperfection

 Predictive Protection

 Engineered Addiction

 Small Data

 Disruptive Distribution

 Micro Consumption

 ## EVERYDAY STARDOM

The growth of personalization leads more consumers to expect everyday interactions to be transformed into celebrity experiences with them as the stars of the show.

Trend Longevity Rating

As companies use big data to personalize experiences and revamp customers' experience, consumers' expectations rise, sometimes verging on the impossible.

 ## SELFIE CONFIDENCE

The ability to share a carefully crafted online persona allows people to use selfies to build their own self-esteem and confidence by portraying themselves as they wish to be seen in the world.

Trend Longevity Rating

The essence of this trend remains unchanged, but how we portray ourselves online or build our confidence has moved far beyond , as you can read in the megatrend of *Amplified Identity*.

 ## MAINSTREAM MINDFULNESS

Meditation, yoga, and quiet contemplation become powerful tools for individuals and organizations to improve performance, health, and motivation.

Trend Longevity Rating

Not only did we bring this trend back as a featured trend in 2017, but it has come to describe entire industries, new ways of thinking, and a strong movement to improve ourselves at home and at work.

BRANDED BENEVOLENCE

Companies increasingly put purpose at the center of their businesses to show a deeper commitment to doing good that goes beyond donating money or getting positive PR.

Trend Longevity Rating A-

This was the first of our trends to spotlight brands demonstrating a commitment to the environment, social issues, and ethical business practices, a theme that is discussed in the *Purposeful Profit* megatrend.

 ## GLANCEABLE CONTENT

Our shrinking attention spans and the explosion of all forms of content online and offline lead creators to optimize stories for rapid consumption at a glance.

Trend Longevity Rating B

Daily or hourly content keeps attracting attention and is appealing because it is quickly scanned. However, it is a double-edged sword as it pushes makers toward creating a spectacle.

 ## REVERSE RETAIL

Brands increasingly invest in high-touch in-store experiences to build brand affinity and educate customers, while seamlessly integrating online channels to complete actual purchases and fulfill orders.

Trend Longevity Rating A-

Since this trend first was published, retailers have continued to focus on being experiential and immersive, a fact we further explored in our 2019 trend of *Strategic Spectacle*.

 ## MOOD MATCHING

As tracking technology becomes more sophisticated, media, advertising, and immersive experiences like gaming and learning can be tailored to match consumer moods.

Trend Longevity Rating A

As new technology such as the use of facial tracking AI becomes more widespread, the idea that you can be engaged or marketed to based on your mood is likely to gain more traction.

 ## RELUCTANT MARKETER

As marketing shifts away from pure promotion, leaders and organizations abandon traditional silos, embrace content marketing, and invest in the customer experience.

Trend Longevity Rating B

Marketing continues to evolve away from promotion and to incorporate lessons from sales, innovation, research, data, and more, which leads to marketers' reluctance about what to call themselves.

 ## EXPERIMEDIA

Content creators use social experiments and real-life interactions to study human behavior in unique new ways and ultimately to build more realistic and entertaining narratives.

Trend Longevity Rating B-

It once seemed that media featuring social experiments would continue indefinitely, but this trend has slowed as the popularity of viral experiments to shock and awe wanes.

UNPERFECTION

As people seek more personal and human experiences, brands and creators intentionally focus on personality, quirkiness, and intentional imperfections to be more human and desirable.

Trend Longevity Rating

The idea that brands and leaders are showing vulnerability and building trust through a willingness to share flaws continues to resonate and is a key ingredient in acting more human.

SMALL DATA

As consumers increasingly collect their own data from online activities, brand-owned big data becomes less valuable than small data in certain situations.

Trend Longevity Rating

The potential of small data to help customize experiences is vast, yet it remains underutilized and difficult to leverage in a meaningful way even though we still collect a lot of it.

PREDICTIVE PROTECTION

A growing concern for privacy coupled with elevated expectations of technology's role in our lives leads to more intuitive products, services, and features to help us live better, safer, and more efficient lives.

Trend Longevity Rating

This trend is a precursor to our megatrend of *Protective Tech* and offered an early look at the importance of this type of intuition, an idea we also explore in our 2017 trend of *Robot Renaissance*.

DISRUPTIVE DISTRIBUTION

Creators and makers use new models for distribution to disrupt the usual channels, cut out middlemen, and build more direct connections with fans and buyers.

Trend Longevity Rating

This trend has exploded in recent years and is likely to affect even more industries. It is a central concept that we brought back in 2018 and was a driver of the megatrend *Flux Commerce*.

ENGINEERED ADDICTION

Greater understanding of the behavioral science behind habit formation leads to more designers and engineers intentionally creating addictive experiences that capture consumers' time, money, and loyalty.

Trend Longevity Rating

If you consider the growth of everything from packaged foods to fantasy sports, this trend is central to how experiences can be engineered to be irresistible whether they are good for us or not.

MICRO CONSUMPTION

As new payment models, products, and experiences become available in bite-sized portions, multiple industries will experiment with new micro-sized forms of pricing and payments.

Trend Longevity Rating

This trend continues to show huge potential. Unfortunately, platforms still quibble over micro-currency formats. It remains difficult to use, and microtransactions aren't mainstream.

THE 2016 NON-OBVIOUS TREND REPORT OVERVIEW

Originally published January 25, 2016
Original Format: Paperback + ebook

The Backstory + Retrospective

After releasing the book in print for the first time in 2015, it was tempting to return to digital for the new editions. The volume of my in-person appearances made this impractical, so I chose to publish a paperback update to the book less than 12 months after the original was released. The update followed the convention of previous years by introducing new trends. However, given the compressed time frame, my growing team and I realized that we might abandon some predictions before we explored their significance.

As a result, we decided on a new convention: Every year moving forward, we would curate ten new trends and renew five previous predictions with an update on how those trends had evolved since we first wrote about them.

In the 2016 edition, readers were introduced to the new ideas of *Strategic Downgrading*, about consumers choosing supposedly inferior earlier versions of products because they often worked better, lasted longer, or were easier to use; *Automated Adulthood,* on the growing range of technology making things easier for young people launching their independent lives; and *Virtual Empathy,* about the idea that technology might offer us a path to empathy for others unlike ourselves.

For the first and only time, the book included an ill-advised 2016 update in which each trend from the previous year was revisited with more examples. Most readers thought it was not essential and unnecessarily long. In future editions, we relied instead on a final section similar to this one to analyze past predictions.

2016 TRENDS AT A GLANCE

 E-mpulse Buying

 Strategic Downgrading

 Optimistic Aging

 B2Beyond Marketing

 Personality Mapping

 Branded Utility

 Mainstream Multiculturalism

 Earned Consumption

 Anti-stereotyping

 Virtual Empathy

 Data Overflow

 Heroic Design

 Insourced Incubation

 Automated Adulthood

 Obsessive Productivity

E-MPULSE BUYING

Despite fears that the e-commerce might kill impulse buying, real-time marketing and smart interfaces entice consumers to make split-second emotional buying decisions online as well.

Trend Longevity Rating A

As the sophistication of e-commerce grows, online selling is offering more opportunities to encourage impulse buys through upselling, retargeting, bundling, and many other techniques.

STRATEGIC DOWNGRADING

As more products and services get upgraded, consumers start rejecting these supposedly improved options and downgrading to simpler, cheaper, and more functional versions.

Trend Longevity Rating A

Since first writing about this trend, it has taken on a life of its own across the Internet. Consumers continue to seek simplicity, choose retro products, and reject excessive options.

OPTIMISTIC AGING

(Originally curated 2013)

After years of being sold anti-aging solutions, a generation of newly aging adults are embracing the upside of getting older and finding optimism in the time their "third age" can offer.

Trend Longevity Rating B

This optimism about the future remains intact. However, it is tempered by rising fears about the environment, divisive politics, and a global economy in flux.

B2BEYOND MARKETING

B2B brands embrace their humanity, take inspiration from other sectors, and think more broadly about effectively marketing to decision makers as people first and niche B2B buyers second.

Trend Longevity Rating

This was one of those frustrating trends that were well predicted and quantifiably true, yet it struggled to accelerate because so many B2B brands resist different thinking.

PERSONALITY MAPPING

As behavioral measurement tools build a detailed map of our personalities, organizations can use this information to bring like-minded people together and more effectively engage them.

Trend Longevity Rating

This trend had a high potential to engage people based on what they love, but in the past few years, it was wasted by overly segmenting audiences or trying to sell them something.

BRANDED UTILITY

(Originally curated 2014)

Brands begin to focus on a combination of content marketing and a greater integration between marketing and operations to provide value through usefulness in customer's lives.

Trend Longevity Rating A

As content marketing continues to grow, brands increasingly find new ways to provide value, answer questions, and use marketing as a tool for education rather than purely for promotion.

MAINSTREAM MULTICULTURALISM

After years of being ignored, niche demographics, multicultural citizens, and their cultures find widespread acceptance through a growing integration of diverse ideas in culture and media.

Trend Longevity Rating

Though this trend continues to receive unsettling opposition from small-minded xenophobic politicians, there is an unstoppable generational shift towards acceptance and embrace of multiple cultures.

EARNED CONSUMPTION

The desire for authentic experiences makes consumers more willing to earn their right to consume, offering businesses a chance to build more loyalty and engagement by letting consumers "pay" them.

Trend Longevity Rating B

The quest for status and recognition continues to entice consumers and can be rewarding for the right brands, but it remains a difficult task to stay worthy of this type of customer devotion.

ANTI-STEREOTYPING

(Originally curated 2014)

Across media and entertainment, gender roles start to reverse, assumptions about alternative lifestyles are challenged, diversity increases, and perceptions of how people are defined continue to evolve.

Trend Longevity Rating A-

We continue to see new stories that help us re-evaluate people, see gender as fluid, and generally challenge our long-held assumptions about identity and a blurring of what were once distinct lines.

VIRTUAL EMPATHY

The dramatic growth of virtual reality and immersive technology allows creators to tell deeper stories and lets people see the world from another point of view, growing their empathy for those unlike themselves.

Trend Longevity Rating **A**

The examples of virtual reality and tech used to improve and quantify human empathy have become too numerous to count. This trend was so popular that we brought it back in 2018.

DATA OVERFLOW

The growing amount of personal and corporate-owned data mixed with open data creates new challenges for better automated analysis tools, more AI, smarter curation, and more startup investment.

Trend Longevity Rating **A**

This is the first of a host of data-related trends from 2015 to 2019 that focus on the good and bad of data. A clear "bad" driving the continued relevance of this trend: There is too much of it.

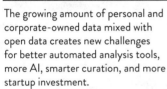

HEROIC DESIGN

(Originally curated 2014)

Design takes a leading role in the introduction of new products, ideas, and inspiration to change the world in nuanced, audacious, irreverent, and sometimes unexpectedly heroic ways.

Trend Longevity Rating **A**

The growth of design thinking and a continued global need for audacious solutions to problems facing humankind have made this a trend we see renewed examples of every year.

INSOURCED INCUBATION

Companies desperate to be more innovative increasingly look to bring more outside innovators in-house, enticing them with funding, beautiful co-working lab spaces, and a feel-good pitch.

Trend Longevity Rating **B-**

While this activity remained popular for few years, limited results and an outsized focus on the theater of innovation led to a slowdown, a point we noted in 2019 trend *Innovation Envy*.

AUTOMATED ADULTHOOD

As more people go through a prolonged period of emerging adulthood, a growing range of technology and services helps to automate all aspects of their journey to adulthood.

Trend Longevity Rating **A**

New tools for automated living, smart homes, and predictive tech are combining with co-living options to help softly guide emerging adults emotionally and physically into becoming somewhat fully independent.

OBSESSIVE PRODUCTIVITY

(Originally curated 2014)

Thanks to our reduced attention spans and always-on technology, the necessity to be productive in every moment rapidly evolved into an obsession that underpins every moment.

Trend Longevity Rating **A**

More than three years after this trend was curated, people continue to fret over productivity, hack their time, and desperately seek to save time through any means possible.

THE 2017 NON-OBVIOUS
TREND REPORT OVERVIEW

Originally published December 5, 2016
Original Format: Paperback + ebook

The Backstory + Retrospective

If you ever looked at purchasing a new model of a car, you know that manufacturers don't revamp the entire design every year. Some years the model is relatively unchanged, and some years it is updated significantly. This was a "maintenance" year for the Non-Obvious Trend series: The interior design and format were largely the same as 2016. The book again had a big release, and for the first time it was distributed widely across desirable locations, such as airport bookstores, which helped broaden the audience.

More readers discovered the report for the first time, and more international translations entered the market. Meanwhile, my speaking dates and workshops continued to grow. From a content perspective, this was a popular year with several standout trends, including *Passive Loyalty*, about a shift in how brands actually gain loyalty; *Fierce Femininity*, on the new revolution in how women are portrayed in media and culture; and *Invisible Technology*, about how technology increasingly anticipates our needs and blends unnoticeably into our lives.

This 2017 edition also won the first of what would be many book honors, a Silver Medal for Business Theory from the highly competitive Axiom Book Awards.

2017 TRENDS AT A GLANCE

 Fierce Femininity

 Side Quirks

 Desperate Detox

 Passive Loyalty

 Authentic Fameseekers

 Lovable Unperfection

 Preserved Past

 Deep Diving

 Precious Print

 Invisible Technology

 Robot Renaissance

 Self-Aware Data

 Moonshot Entrepreneurship

 Outrageous Outsiders

Mainstream Mindfulness

FIERCE FEMININITY

The fierce, independent woman has emerged in recent years, redefining the concept of femininity and reimagining gender roles.

Trend Longevity Rating

Current events and the political and cultural climate continue to shift how we perceive women's place in modern society. Since publishing this trend, we see a new story reinforcing its validity almost weekly.

SIDE QUIRKS

A global shift toward individualism has led to a surge in side-hustle, entrepreneurs driven by passion, and a renewed appreciation for what makes people unique.

Trend Longevity Rating

People continue to create value from their hobbies, passions, and personality quirks. This desire to pursue side projects and the global rise of individualism inspired us to bring this trend back in 2019.

DESPERATE DETOX

(Originally curated 2014)

As technology, media clutter, and an overload of gadgets make life increasingly stressful, people are seeking moments of reflection and pause.

Trend Longevity Rating

Tech saturation continues to drive people to find a respite. Apps help people to disconnect, places in the real world offer tech-free zones, and people seek more peace and quiet.

PASSIVE LOYALTY

A new understanding of loyalty is challenging brands to get smarter about how they can generate brand enthusiasts.

Trend Longevity Rating **A**

Forward-looking brands redesign their loyalty programs and try delight to inspire loyalty. Given the focus on this, we decided to republish this trend in 2019.

 ## PRESERVED PAST

(Originally curated 2014)

Technology is offering new ways to preserve history, changing the way we experience, remember, and learn from the past in the process.

Trend Longevity Rating **A**

This trend continues to be vitally important as work continues to preserve artifacts digitally and produce 3D libraries of cultural sites before they are damaged in war or consumed by natural disaster.

 ## AUTHENTIC FAMESEEKERS

A new generation of creators is turning to social media to establish brands, attract eyeballs, and become the next big thing.

Trend Longevity Rating **B**

Influencers continue to be a force online, but their constant quest to capture our attention is leading to fatigue with their supposed authenticity and diverting attention elsewhere.

 ## DEEP DIVING

While brands compete for our shrinking attention spans with more content than ever, many people prefer to go all in on the topics and experiences that truly capture their interest.

Trend Longevity Rating **A**

People still find enjoyment in content and storytelling that takes them deep into interesting topics. Podcasts, investigative journalism, immersive film, and other long-form experiences continue to be appealing.

 ## LOVABLE UNPERFECTION

(Originally curated 2014)

Today successful marketing campaigns increasing focus on using the power of personality, quirkiness, and imperfections to create authentic with customers connections.

Trend Longevity Rating **A**

The idea that brands and leaders are showing vulnerability and building trust through a willingness to share flaws continues to resonate and is a key ingredient in brands acting more human.

 ## PRECIOUS PRINT

(Originally curated 2013)

Thanks to the digital revolution, people are developing a more meaningful and emotional relationship with physical objects and printed material.

Trend Longevity Rating **A**

The fact that we place even more value on the things that are printed because they are more valuable and rarer has continued, leading us to integrate this trend into the 2018 trend of *Touchworthy*.

INVISIBLE TECHNOLOGY

As technology grows more sophisticated, it becomes better at predicting and anticipating needs, protecting us, and providing utility while blending seamlessly into our lives.

Trend Longevity Rating

Technology continues seamlessly to make everyday tasks and transactions easier, cheaper, and more efficient. These benefits make this trend continually relevant and a key element of our *Protective Tech* megatrend.

MOONSHOT ENTREPRENEURSHIP

A new generation of entrepreneurs is thinking beyond profit and placing social impact, not financial performance, at the center of their organizations' missions.

Trend Longevity Rating

The world's problems remain complex, and entrepreneurs generate social impact and fill the gap left by ineffective governments. This trend also inspired the trend of *Good Speed* from the 2019 report.

ROBOT RENAISSANCE

As robots' utility moves into the home and the workplace, they adopt more human-like interfaces and micro-personalities.

Trend Longevity Rating

As we live through this "renaissance age" of robots, we are tackling big questions about what we want them to do and what we don't. The debate and trend could shape the decade to come.

OUTRAGEOUS OUTSIDERS

Some of today's most innovative and influential ideas are coming from complete outsiders whose unconventional quirks disrupt entire industries.

Trend Longevity Rating

Outsiders continue to disrupt entire industries, countries, and global orders. We expect this trend will continue to affect everything from politics to music in the coming decade.

SELF-AWARE DATA

As technology advances, algorithms and artificial intelligence make real-time analysis so fast that it can move from input to insight to action all on its own.

Trend Longevity Rating

In contrast to our more alarmist trends of *Data Overflow* and *Data Pollution*, this trend suggests data might create value by analyzing itself — something that is showing signs of happening.

MAINSTREAM MINDFULNESS

(Originally curated 2015)

Meditation, yoga, and quiet contemplation become powerful tools for individuals and organizations to improve performance, health, and motivation.

Trend Longevity Rating

Since the trend was predicted several years ago, it has continued to describe entire industries, new ways of thinking, and a strong movement to improve ourselves at home and at work.

THE 2018 NON-OBVIOUS
TREND REPORT OVERVIEW

Originally published December 5, 2017
Original Format: Paperback + ebook

The Backstory + Retrospective

For this edition, I engaged a completely new team and introduced an upgraded and more visual interior design. The book incorporated more photographs and a unique color on the inside to add contrast.

Some of the most popular trends from this report included *Truthing,* about why we trust in face-to-face interactions more than any other type; *Brand Stand,* on why consumers buy from brands who are unafraid to share what they believe in; *Light-Speed Learning,* about why we expect to learn anything faster than ever; and *Manipulated Outrage,* on what happens when a news media culture of outrage starts to define an individual's identity.

Thanks in part to the updates, as well as submissions to many more industry book awards, the 2018 edition won six additional business book honors, including selection as a finalist for the prestigious Leonard L. Berry Marketing Book Prize from the American Marketing Association.

2018 TRENDS AT A GLANCE

 Truthing

 Ungendered

 Enlightened Consumption

 Overtargeting

 Brand Stand

 Backstorytelling

 Manipulated Outrage

 Light-speed Learning

 Virtual Empathy

 Human Mode

 Data Pollution

 Predictive Protection

 Approachable Luxury

Touchworthy

Disruptive Distribution

TRUTHING

With trust eroding in media and institutions, people are engaging in a personal quest for the truth based on direct observation and face-to-face interaction.

Trend Longevity Rating

As distrust of the media, governments, and corporations spreads, this important trend describes a critical coping mechanism of looking inward that shows no sign of stopping.

UNGENDERED

Shifting definitions of traditional gender roles are leading some to reject the notion of gender completely, while others aim to mask gender from products, experiences, and even their own identities.

Trend Longevity Rating

This trend not only has grown so quickly, but also has been so culture changing and defining that we selected a slightly redefined and elevated version of it as one of our megatrends, *Ungendering*.

ENLIGHTENED CONSUMPTION

Empowered with information about products and services, people are choosing to make a statement about their values and the world through what they buy, where they work, and how they invest.

Trend Longevity Rating

This is a critical trend to watch because of the speed with which we access to real-time information to evaluate the impact our buying has on the world.

OVERTARGETING

Lured by the promise of big data, organizations segment audiences too narrowly and unintentionally end up abandoning large groups of potentially lucrative customers.

Trend Longevity Rating **B**

While businesses frequently and unnecessarily narrow their audience, in many cases it has not raised the major issues or challenges that we initially predicted.

MANIPULATED OUTRAGE

Media, data analytics, and advertising are combining forces to create a perpetual stream of noise that is intended to incite rage and elicit angry reactions on social media and in real life.

Trend Longevity Rating **A**

This trend remains sadly important because of continued manipulation by evil corporations and self-centered politicians. It's exacerbated by gullible media who help amplify the manipulation.

BRAND STAND

Reacting to a polarized media atmosphere, more brands feel compelled to take a stand and highlight their core values rather than try to be all things to all people.

Trend Longevity Rating **A**

In the year since this trend was first predicted, there have been many examples of brands utilizing this effect to inspire belief, share their values, and grow loyalty.

LIGHT-SPEED LEARNING

The road to mastery on any topic gets faster through the help of bite-sized learning modules that make education more time efficient, engaging, useful, and fun.

Trend Longevity Rating **A**

This trend has driven real business change and positive results, and it served as one of the primary inspirations for our megatrend of *Instant Knowledge*.

BACKSTORYTELLING

(Originally curated 2013)

Organizations use the power of stories to share their heritage, mission, and reason for existing with audiences. Their aim is to earn loyalty and position themselves as desirable places to work.

Trend Longevity Rating **A**

If there is any trend that could be described as universally important, it would be this one. Though it has been brought back over time, the idea of stories as a way for brands to stand apart continues to be an effective strategy.

VIRTUAL EMPATHY

(Originally curated 2014)

Immersive experiences delivered through technology and personal interactions increase empathy by helping people see the world through foreign and unfamiliar eyes.

Trend Longevity Rating **A**

This trend has broadened beyond virtual reality technology to include examples of installations, art projects, and live experiences that offer people ways to feel more empathy.

HUMAN MODE

As automation increases, people hungry for more personal and authentic experiences begin to put a premium on advice, services, and interaction involving actual humans.

Trend Longevity Rating (A)

While automation grows, we will see a rise in the importance of human interactions and a continued willingness to pay a premium in order to have a real person help you in real life.

APPROACHABLE LUXURY

Luxury is no longer defined by scarcity and privilege, but rather more down-to-earth authentic human experiences that create unforgettable moments worth sharing.

Trend Longevity Rating (A)

Alongside luxury that was approachable was luxury that was even more out of touch, designed for the *Overwealthy*, as described in our 2019 prediction.

DATA POLLUTION

As we create more methods for quantifying the world around us, data are manipulated, contaminated, and sabotaged, making it harder to separate true insights from useless noise.

Trend Longevity Rating (A)

There is no doubt the flood of data is rising, and sorting through it to find what really matters is a serious problem that even smart AI has not been able to solve.

TOUCHWORTHY

Overwhelmed by digital, consumers turn back toward products and experiences that they can touch, feel, and sense to deliver a much-needed sense of calm, simplicity, and humanity.

Trend Longevity Rating (A)

The more digital things are becoming, the more important tactile experiences are. Sometimes we just want a more real and tangible experience that we can hold.

PREDICTIVE PROTECTION

(Originally curated 2015)

Organizations create smarter connected products, services, and features that can protect our safety, health, and environment by anticipating our actions or needs.

Trend Longevity Rating (A)

This trend was a precursor to our megatrend of *Protective Tech*. It returned to the report a second time after initially appearing in the 2015 edition.

DISRUPTIVE DISTRIBUTION

(Originally curated 2015)

Traditional models of distribution get reinvented as businesses of all sizes seek more efficiency, build direct connections with consumers, and rethink their own business models.

Trend Longevity Rating (A)

This trend has exploded in recent years and is likely to impact even more industries since we first predicted it in 2015. It was also a driver for the megatrend of *Flux Commerce*.

THE 2019 NON-OBVIOUS TREND REPORT OVERVIEW

Originally published January 1, 2019
Original Format: Paperback + ebook

The Backstory + Retrospective

Continuing with the design introduced in 2018, this edition featured a similarly visual look and feel. Popular trends from this edition included *Innovation Envy,* about corporations desperately copying one another instead of truly thinking differently; *Muddled Masculinity,* on our shifting cultural understanding of what it means to be a man; *Artificial Influence,* about how we increasingly put our faith in influencers who are fabricated for us; and *Retrotrust,* on why we trust products and brands that we recognize from our past.

This new edition also included custom illustrations, updated visuals, and a comprehensive appendix reviewing all past trends. In terms of visibility, the audience for the report and trends continued to grow and receive worldwide attention across 2019. Several more foreign language editions were published, more translation deals were finalized and I continued to present the insights on larger stages and deliver more frequent talks. Foreshadowing the publication of this Megatrends edition, these presentations more frequently focused on multi-year insights and shifts curated across the past decade instead of just a single year's insights.

2019 TRENDS AT A GLANCE

 Strategic Spectacle

 Muddled Masculinity

 Side Quirks

 Artificial Influence

 Retrotrust

 B2Beyond Marketing

 Fad Fatigue

 Extreme Uncluttering

 Deliberate Downgrading

 Enterprise Empathy

 Innovation Envy

 Robot Renaissance

 Good Speed

 Overwealthy

 Passive Loyalty

STRATEGIC SPECTACLE

Brands and creators intentionally use spectacles to capture attention and drive engagement.

Trend Longevity Rating A

The use of spectacles continues to grow as a trend. The difficulty of capturing attention factored significantly into the definition of megatrend *Attention Wealth*.

MUDDLED MASCULINITY

The rising empowerment of women and re-evaluation of gender are causing widespread confusion and angst about what it means to be a man today.

Trend Longevity Rating A

There have been continual signs since publishing this trend that the confusion is getting more pronounced and in some cases leading to significant re-evaluations of self-identity from men.

SIDE QUIRKS

(Originally curated 2017)
A global shift toward individualism drives people to follow their passion, start a side business, and appreciate quirks in one another.

Trend Longevity Rating A

Since we first published this trend, the world seems to be getting quirkier than ever. Individualism rises, subgenres grow, and many seem to seek and find new ways to express themselves.

ARTIFICIAL INFLUENCE

Creators, corporations, and governments use virtual creations to shift public perception, sell products, and even turn fantasy into reality.

Trend Longevity Rating **B**

While Artificial Influence keeps rising, we are seeing subtle and direct ways that people are fighting back against this manufactured influence and demanding more authenticity.

FAD FATIGUE

Consumers get weary of innovations claiming to be the next big thing and assume none will last long.

Trend Longevity Rating **A**

Perhaps inevitably the speed of innovation and disruption has led to a continued relevance for this trend as people still feel this same fatigue and maintain their skepticism about all fads as a result.

RETROTRUST

Often unsure of whom to trust, consumers look back to organizations and experiences with brands that have a legacy as well as those with which they have a personal history.

Trend Longevity Rating **A**

This trend has plenty of new stories from the year since we initially spotlighted it, and it played a fundamental part in the definition for our megatrend *Revivalism*.

EXTREME UNCLUTTERING

To simplify daily life, people shed their excess stuff and seek pared-down experiences and ways to unclutter their digital identities, too.

Trend Longevity Rating **A**

There are no indications that this sometimes desperate quest to reduce clutter is slowing down. Instead, people seek even more ways to simplify, get rid of "stuff" and declutter their daily lives.

B2BEYOND MARKETING

(Originally curated 2016)

B2B brands use non-traditional methods to embrace their humanity and reach decision makers along with a broader audience.

Trend Longevity Rating **B**

This was one of those frustrating trends that was well predicted and quantifiably true, yet it struggled to accelerate because of the resistance so many B2B brands have to different thinking.

DELIBERATE DOWNGRADING

(Originally curated 2016)

As tech-enabled products become overbearing, consumers opt to downgrade to simpler, cheaper, or more functional versions instead.

Trend Longevity Rating **A**

This trend, slightly revised from the original *Deliberate vs Strategic Downgrading*, continues to be widely cited as consumers skip excessively upgraded options and choose the option they prefer.

ENTERPRISE EMPATHY

Empathy becomes a driver of innovation and revenue as well as a point of differentiation for products, services, hiring, and experiences.

Trend Longevity Rating

An evolution from *Virtual Empathy*, this trend was written to encompass the many businesses now using empathy as a competitive advantage far beyond tech firms pioneering Virtual Reality experiences.

GOOD SPEED

The urgency of the problems facing humanity is inspiring corporations, entrepreneurs, and individuals to find ways of doing good and generating results more quickly.

Trend Longevity Rating

More examples appear of good being done by entrepreneurs and large brands alike as they feel the urgency to make an impact and share it with conscientious consumers who care.

INNOVATION ENVY

Fear leads entrepreneurs, businesses, and institutions to envy competitors and approach innovation with admiration or desperation.

Trend Longevity Rating

This was perhaps the most popular trend of the 2019 report, inspiring corporate leaders to launch internal initiatives to ensure they weren't engaging in some *Innovation Envy* themselves.

OVERWEALTHY

Growing income inequality leads to more guilt among the affluent, prompting them to seek more ways to give back.

Trend Longevity Rating

As income inequality worsens, the affluent try to find ways to help but often fail. Solutions to such large issues continue to evade us. This trend hasn't moved much.

ROBOT RENAISSANCE

(Originally curated 2017)

As robots adopt more human-like interfaces and micro-personalities, they are raising new questions and issues about how we relate to technology.

Trend Longevity Rating

As we live through this "renaissance age" of robots, we are tackling big questions about what we want them to do and what we don't. This debate and trend could shape the decade to come.

PASSIVE LOYALTY

(Originally curated 2017)

As switching from brands becomes easier, companies re-evaluate who is loyal, who isn't, and how to inspire true loyalty.

Trend Longevity Rating

Forward-looking brands redesign their loyalty programs and try delight to inspire loyalty. Given the focus on this, we decided to bring back and republish this trend in 2019.

CONCLUSION

APPARENTLY, THE WORLD WILL END on March 16, 2880.

I came across this fact while putting the final touches on the first edition of Non-Obvious. A team of scientists, I read in a story, discovered a 0.3 percent chance the world will end on that day due to a cosmic collision course between Earth and a celestial body known only as Asteroid 1950 DA.

The story immediately struck me as the perfect example of the types of predictions we commonly encounter today: overblown proclamations of some impending doom and relatively little useful advice on what we can do to change it.

One of the goals of this book is to challenge lazy or obvious ways of thinking that are, sadly, no more useful than these hyperbolic futuristic predictions. In fact, seeing the world in a narrow or one-dimensional way is even more damaging than a doomsday prophecy, because it often leads to people making flawed decisions *today*— not just spreading empty dread for our distant future.

This book intentionally doesn't offer geopolitical arguments for why Denmark is going to become the world's next superpower by 2050 thanks to wind energy production, or sexy guesses about how self-driving, flying cars might enable virtual-reality tourism during daily commutes. These kinds of predictions are fun to write and read. Some might even come true. But most are cloaked in uncertainty.

Predicting our future should involve far less guesswork.

Curating trends is certainly about seeing what others miss. But it's also about developing a mindset of curiosity and thoughtfulness. It's about moving from being a speed reader to being a "speed understander," as Isaac Asimov wrote. The future will belong to these non-obvious thinkers who use their powers of observation to see connections between industries, ideas, and behaviors and curate them into a deeper understanding of the accelerating present.

Can non-obvious thinking save us from an asteroid 867 years from now? I hope so. But more immediately, embracing this way of thinking can change the way we approach our lives and our businesses today. Preparing for the future starts with filtering out the noise and getting better at understanding the present — as it always has.

ACKNOWLEDGEMENTS

THE IDEA FOR THIS book was born ten years ago. Since that humble first report, this decade long project has been inspired by the tens of thousands of people who have debated, challenged and shared every edition of these insights and helped them improve every year—and so these acknowledgements fittingly must start with my gratitude to all of them.

In addition to the readers, every edition of Non-Obvious has also benefitted from a small army of amazingly talented professionals who have helped me transform a pile of papers, handwritten notes and Post-It Notes into the book you're holding in your hands now—and so I would like to offer these special thanks to each of them:

To my intrepid editor Genoveva, who consistently made the arguments in this book smarter, identified gaps in the arguments and offered a detailed read of the book that made it better in every way.

To my extended editorial team including Herb, Christina, Gretchen, Terry, Kay, Michele, Bev, Paresh, Eliza and Matthew for offering an ongoing sounding board of high impact editorial advice—whether they worked on this current book or one of the past editions.

To Frank, Anton, Jessica, Joss, Maureen, Jeff, Kelly, for all your expertise in shaping the visual design of the book and making it such a beautiful read inside and out.

To Marleen, Chrys and the foreign rights team for helping to bring the book to so many new audiences around the world.

To Renee and Katie for helping me bring this message to so many stages throughout the world with keynotes and workshops—I couldn't manage any of those without your support.

To Viveca, Hugo and the full China team for helping to bring these insights, and Non-Obvious thinking, to the Chinese market.

To Marnie for all your work keeping this and so many other Ideapress projects on track.

To Rich for being a great partner, working under a crazy timeline and always getting things done.

To my wife Chhavi, who continually manages to cheerfully deal with a writing process that requires me to sometimes disappear for days to finish off Chapters and "visualize" ideas by spreading my notes across inconvenient areas of the house. As a daily collaborator, she has helped make the arguments stronger, challenged me to think bigger and made the ten-year journey behind this book better in every way. It is easy to imagine the future when you are married to someone who inspires you.

And finally, to my boys Rohan and Jaiden for remaining curious enough about the world to motivate me to observe more, judge less and always listen with both ears.

From time to time, we all need a reminder like that.

BELOW YOU WILL FIND a selected list of some of the books I consulted while writing Non-Obvious Megatrends. Not all of them are cited directly in the endnotes, but they are grouped here based on the chapter for which their insights are most relevant—and they are all highly recommended.

INTRODUCTION

The Next 100 Years: A Forecast for the 21st Century
by George Friedman

Up the Organization: How to Stop the Corporation from Stifling People and Strangling Profits
by Robert Townsend

It's Been a Good Life
by Isaac Asimov and Janet Jeppson Asimov

CHAPTER 1

Mindset: The New Psychology of Success
by Carol Dweck

The Sense of Style: The Thinking Person's Guide to Writing in the 21st Century
by Steven Pinker

The Laws of Simplicity (Simplicity: Design, Technology, Business, Life)
by John Maeda

Back of the Napkin: Solving Problems and Selling Ideas with Pictures
by Dan Roam

How to Make Sense of Any Mess: Information Architecture for Everybody
by Abby Covert

CHAPTER 2

CHAPTER 3

CHAPTER 4—AMPLIFIED IDENTITY

CHAPTER 5—UNGENDERING

Delusions of Gender: How Our Minds, Society, and Neurosexism Create Difference
by Cordelia Fine

We Should All Be Feminists
by Chimamanda Ngozi Adichie

Otherhood: Modern Women Finding A New Kind of Happiness
by Melanie Notkin

The Athena Doctrine: How Women (and the Men Who Think Like Them) Will Rule the Future
by John Gerzema and Michael D'Antonio

Bad Feminist: Essays
by Roxane Gay

The Madness of Crowds: Gender, Race and Identity
by Douglas Murray

CHAPTER 6—INSTANT KNOWLEDGE

College (Un)bound: The Future of Higher Education and What It Means for Students
by Jeffrey J. Selingo

How We Learn: The Surprising Truth About When, Where, and Why It Happens
by Benedict Carey

Education That Works: The Neuroscience of Building a More Effective Higher Education
by Dr. James Stellar

Ultralearning: Master Hard Skills, Outsmart the Competition, and Accelerate Your Career
by Scott H. Young

End of College: Creating the Future of Learning and University of Everywhere
by Kevin Carey

Leveraged Learning: How the Disruption of Education Helps Lifelong Learners, and Experts with Something to Teach
by Danny Iny

CHAPTER 7—ATTENTION WEALTH

The Attention Merchants: The Epic Scramble to Get Inside Our Heads
by Tim Wu

Trust Me, I'm Lying: Confessions of a Media Manipulator
by Ryan Holiday

Weaponized Lies: How to Think Critically in the Post-Truth Era
by Daniel J. Levitin

The Persuaders: The Hidden Industry That Wants to Change Your Mind
by James Garvey

Brandwashed: Tricks Companies Use to Manipulate Our Minds and Persuade Us to Buy
by Martin Lindstrom

Savvy: Navigating Fake Companies, Fake Leaders and Fake News in the Post-Trust Era
by Shiv Singh and Rohini Luthra

CHAPTER 8—REVIVALISM

The Revenge of Analog: Real Things and Why They Matter
by David Sax

Words Onscreen: The Fate of Reading in a Digital World
by Naomi S. Baron

Digital Minimalism: Choosing a Focused Life in a Noisy World
by Cal Newport

The Missing Ink: The Lost Art of Handwriting
by Philip Hensher

Shop Class as Soulcraft: An Inquiry into the Value of Work
by Matthew B. Crawford

A Craftsman's Legacy: Why Working with Our Hands Gives Us Meaning
by Eric Gorges and Jon Sternfeld

CHAPTER 9—HUMAN MODE

Alone Together: Why We Expect More from Technology and Less from Each Other
by Sherri Turkle

Empathy: Why It Matters and How to Get It
by Roman Krznaric

The Empathy Effect: Seven Neuroscience-Based Keys for Transforming the Way We Live, Love, Work, and Connect across Differences
by Helen Riess

Messy: The Power of Disorder to Transform Our Lives
by Tim Harford

CHAPTER 10—PURPOSEFUL PROFIT

Conscious Capitalism: Liberating the Heroic Spirit of Business
by John Mackey and Raj Sisodia

People, Power, and Profits: Progressive Capitalism for an Age of Discontent
by Joseph E. Stiglitz

Do Good: Embracing Brand Citizenship to Fuel Both Purpose and Profit
by Anne Bahr Thompson

Winners Take All: The Elite Charade of Changing the World
by Anand Giridharadas

Let My People Go Surfing: The Education of a Reluctant Businessman—Including 10 More Years of Business Unusual
by Yvon Chouinard

Delivering Happiness: A Path to Profits, Passion, and Purpose
by Tony Hsieh

CHAPTER 11—PROTECTIVE TECH

Rise of the Robots: Technology and the Threat of a Jobless Future
by Martin Ford

Automating Inequality: How High-Tech Tools Profile, Police, and Punish the Poor
by Virginia Eubanks

Life 3.0: Being Human in the Age of Artificial Intelligence
by Max Tegmark

The Inevitable: Understanding the 12 Technological Forces That Will Shape Our Future
by Kevin Kelly

Overcomplicated: Technology at the Limits of Comprehension
by Samuel Arbesman

CHAPTER 12—DATA ABUNDANCE

Weapons of Math Destruction: How Big Data Increases Inequality and Threatens Democracy
by Cathy O'Neil

Dataclysm: Love, Sex, Race, and Identity--What Our Online Lives Tell Us about Our Offline Selves
by Christian Rudder

The Signal and the Noise: Why So Many Predictions Fail--but Some Don't
by Nate Silver

NOTES

THE PROCESS OF CURATING the megatrends presented in this book has involved reading tens of thousands of articles and hundreds of books. We have conducted dozens of interviews and benefited from the insights of thousands of readers. In this section, you will see an abbreviated list of the sources we cited in the book along with details for further reading.

INTRODUCTION

Page 3 Paula Green. This story is collected from a number of sources, including an article from Slate and a video interview recorded with Green during a Google Project where she was consulted to help bring the campaign back to life for Avis in 2012:
- Seth Stevenson, "We're No. 2! We're No. 2! How a Mad Men—era ad firm discovered the perks of being an underdog," *Slate, August 12, 2013.*
- *"Project Re: Brief—Paula Green—Re-imagining Avis, "We Try Harder,"* Google, April 12, 2012. Watch the full video at https://www.youtube.com/watch?v=QamKVlqoh5Q

Page 4 "reluctantly agrees to run the campaign." This story comes from the opening of Townsend's bestselling book Up the Organization: How to Stop the Corporation from Stifling People and Strangling Profits (Knopf, 1970).

Page 6 Asimov's renowned intellect. A story shared in his posthumous autobiography (It's Been a Good Life, pg. 177) mentions that during a conversation over a drink after a panel discussion, novelist Kurt Vonnegut once asked Asimov, "How does it feel to know everything?" Asimov replied, "I only know how it feels to have the reputation of knowing everything. Uneasy."

Page 6 "nearly 500 books." A complete list of Asimov's published works ranges from 468 to 506 books, depending on whether you count books that included letters Asimov wrote before his death but which were published posthumously. A full list of his published books can be found online at http://www.asimovonline.com/oldsite/asimov_titles.html

Page 6 Watching TV on fast forward. http://www.washingtonpost.com/news/wonk/wp/2016/06/22/i-have-found-a-new-way-to-watch-tv-and-it-changes-everything/

Page 6 Speed reading apps. https://www.lifewire.com/best-speed-reading-apps-4137047

Page 6 Time hacking methods. https://hackernoon.com/the-time-hacker-method-12970c47f04f

Page 8 Mini Bottle Gallery. This story is gathered from firsthand conversations with staff at the gallery, stories available online about the founding, and literature provided to visitors at the museum.

Page 9 The Non-Obvious Trend Report (2011). You can still read the entire first trend report as it was originally published at www.nonobvious.com/trends/

CHAPTER 1

Page 14 parking ticket, not a car wreck. Dweck's Mindset is filled with analogies and anecdotes like this one to illustrate the value of a growth mindset versus a fixed one. (Mindset, pg. 9)

Page 16 The truth about Columbus. Columbus deserves little of the ceremony he gets and, in fact, he never even set foot in North America during his infamous journey in 1492. Listen to the full story: http://www.npr.org/templates/story/story.php?storyId=141164702

Page 16 Curse of knowledge. The famous linguist Steven Pinker discusses this "curse of knowledge" in his book The Sense of Style, where he notes that the more expertise we have about a topic, the more difficult we tend to find it to simplify or explain it to those who are not as well versed as ourselves.

Page 24 Jeff Karp + Bioinspiration. Josh Cassidy & Laura Shields, "Porcupine Barbs For Better Wound Healing," *NPR*, April 9, 2019.

CHAPTER 2

Page 27 crystal ball. This endorsement was from Bob Ingle at the Atlanta Journal Constitution and cited among the early praise and endorsements section at the beginning of the Megatrends paperback (Warner Books edition, 1984)

Page 28 John Naisbitt Interview. *USA Today*, September 24, 2006.

Page 46 Dong Nguyen and Flappy Bird. David Kushner, "The Flight of the Birdman: Flappy Bird Creator Dong Nguyen Speaks Out," *Rolling Stone*, March 11, 2014.

Page 47 Bliss point. Michael Moss is a Pulitzer Prize–winning investigative journalist. For a short summary of his story on the scientists who uncovered and exploited the "bliss point," see this excerpt from his book reprinted in the New York Times, February 24, 2013:

Page 48 Addicted by Design. In her book, Schüll explores the idea of a trance-like state she calls the "machine zone," where gambling addicts play not to win but simply to keep playing. When this machine design is combined with casinos' focus on "ambience management," addiction is the result.

CHAPTER 3

Page 51 RumChata popularity. Interview with Jim Cramer, "RumChata founder on reaching millennials with the No. 1 spirit brand on social media," *CNBC Mad Money*, September 15, 2017.

Page 53 "How carrots became the new junk food." Douglas McGray, "How Carrots Became The New Junk Food," *Fast Company*, March 22, 2001.

Page 60 Petter Neby and Punkt. Vlad Savov, "The Punkt MP02 is Android minimalism at its finest," *The Verge*, March 1, 2019.

CHAPTER 4—AMPLIFIED IDENTITY

Page 71 "hikikomori." Laurence Butet-Roch, "Pictures Reveal the Isolated Lives of Japan's Social Recluses," *National Geographic*, February 14, 2018.

Page 71 "wangda." Korea Herald, "Growth of the 'Me-Time' Generation," *Star Online*, September 25, 2016.

Page 72 "rising shift toward individualism." "Individualistic Practices and Values Increasing around the World," news release, Association for Psychological Science, n.d.

Page 72 "amplified sense of the importance of the 'self.'" Amanda Cassidy, "The Startling Rise of the Narcissist and How to Recognise the Signs," *Image*, August 3, 2019.

Page 72 "fell to their deaths." Suz, "Understanding the Multiple Horseshoe Bend Deaths and What to Do in Page, Arizona Instead," theobriensabroad.com, October 23, 2019.

Page 73 "you had to be a better you." Will Storr, *Selfie* (London: Picador, 2017), 256.

Page 73 "tiny pulse of girl pride." Rachel Simmons, "Selfies Are Good for Girls," *Slate*, November 20, 2013.

Page 74 "accountability." Diane Aguilera, "The Truth about Online Lying," *Stanford Magazine*, September 2018.

Page 74 "students seem to be less deceptive." Caitlin Hayes, "How Social Media Affects Our Wellbeing," *Cornell Research*, n.d.

Page 74 "Dale Carnegie once wrote." Though his quote is widely known, the story behind Carnegie's rise and how his ideas became mainstream only after he had been teaching his course for 24 years is a fascinating story that is recounted in this biography: Giles Kemp and Edward Claflin, *Dale Carnegie: The Man Who Influenced Millions* (New York: St. Martin's Press, 1989). I also retold this story in the opening of my book *Likeonomics*.

Page 75 "performances of a fantasy wedding." Shobita Dhar, "The Matrimony Matinee," *Times of India*

Page 75 "unboxing toys." Heather Kelly, "The Bizarre, Lucrative World of 'Unboxing' Videos," *CNN Business*, February 13, 2014.

Page 75 "anointed 'influencers.'" Bridget March, "How Influencer Beauty Lines Became as Big as Celebrity Collections," *Harpers Bazaar*, February 22, 2019.

Page 75 "attention has become a commodity." danah boyd, "Hacking the Attention Economy," *Points*, Data and Society Research Institute, January 5, 2017.

Page 75 "cyberbullying is all too common." danah boyd and Alice Marwick, "Bullying as True Drama," *New York Times*, September 22, 2011.

Page 76 "defining the boundaries of normality." Jon Ronson, *So You've Been Publicly Shamed* (New York: Riverhead Books, 2015), 269.

Page 76 "Deep fakes." Editorial Board, "Deepfakes Are Dangerous—and They Target a Huge Weakness," *Washington Post*, June 16, 2019.

Page 76 "re-creation algorithms." Dan Robitzski, "The Digital Afterlife Is Open for Business: But It Needs Rules," futurism.com, April 18, 2018.

Page 76 "holograms of public figures." "How Dead Celebrities Are Being Created as Realistic Holograms," *Wired*, May 10, 2018.

Page 76 "America's new obsession." Julia Emmanuele, "Meet the Keswanis, the Family That's About to Become Your New Obsession," *People*, October 30, 2015.

Page 77 "rise of xenophobia." Simon Tisdall, "Rise of Xenophobia Is Fanning Immigration Flames in EU and US," *Guardian*, June 22, 2018.

Page 77 "racial prejudice . . . actually went down." Isaac Stanley-Becker, "Racial Prejudice Has Declined as a Reaction to Trump's Presidency, a New Study Suggests," *Washington Post*, May 24, 2019.

Page 77 "The World Values Survey found." Charles Kenny, "The Data Are In: Young People Are Increasingly Less Racist Than Old People," *Quartz*, May 24, 2017.

CHAPTER 5—UNGENDERING

Page 81 "The Personality Project." You can read more about the project and see the full e-book with 40 contributors at www.rohitbhargava.com/personalityproject.

Page 82 "[Facebook's] free-form [gender] field." Facebook Diversity, Facebook, February 26, 2015,

Page 82 "documentary film about gender." Katie Couric, "What I Learned from 'Gender Revolution,'" *Huffpost*, February 16, 2017.

Page 83 "words used to describe gender are expanding." Kasandra Brabaw, "54 Gender Identity Terms Every Ally Should Know," *Refinery29*, May 31, 2019.

Page 83 "strong leading women." Lily Rothman, "Butt-Kicking Teenage Girls: Coming Soon to a Theater Near You," *Time*, March 27, 2014.

Page 83 Shepherd Laughlin, "Study: Generation Z and Gender," J. Walter Thompson Intelligence, May 20, 2015.

Page 83 "personal transformations." Arielle Bernstein, "What Women Want: How *Orange Is the New Black* Changed Female Narratives," *Irish Times*, July 26, 2019.

Page 83 "Priya's Shakti." Ram Devineni, Lina Srivastava, and Dan Goldman, *Priya's Shakti* (2014)

Page 83 "men had been fired." Audrey Carlson, Maya Salam, Claire Cain Miller, Denise Lu, Ash Ngu, Jugal K. Patel, and Zach Wichter, "#MeToo Brought Down 201 Powerful Men. Nearly Half of Their Replacements Are Women," *New York Times*, October 29, 2018.

Page 83 "finding their empowerment." Elizabeth Blair, "The Fierce Female Characters of Film in 2018," npr.org, December 27, 2018.

Page 84 "circumstantial infertility." Jacoba Urist, "The Otherhood: Single Women Face 'Circumstantial Infertility,'" *Today*, March 4, 2014.

Page 84 "getting married later." Vera Wang and Kim Parker, "Record Share of Americans Have Never Married," Pew Research Center, September 24, 20124.

Page 84 "boys read until about age 12." Elizabeth Mehren, "Publishing's Queen of the Teen Romance Finds Success with a Formula," *Los Angeles Times*, April 20, 1986.

Page 85 "men's thinking on masculinity." Ella Koeze and Anna Maria Barry-Jester, "What Do Men Think It Means to Be a Man?" *Five Thirty Eight*, June 20, 2016.

Page 85 "only one way to be a boy." Sarah Rich, "Today's Masculinity Is Stifling, " *Atlantic*, June 11, 2018.

Page 86 **"out of touch with modern family dynamics."** "The Evolution of Fatherhood: Meet Dad 2.0," mdgadvertising.com, June 16, 2017.

Page 86 **"equipment manager of the household."** Bryce Covert, "Football Player Breaks Gender Norms in Tide Ad," thinkprogress.org, November 19, 2013.

Page 86 **"expected to be the primary family provider."** Gretchen Livingstone and Kim Parker, "Eight Facts about American Dads," Pew Research Center, June 12, 2019.

Page 86 **"mothers are disproportionately expected."** Alison Escalante, "Why Millions of Mothers Are Overwhelmed by Stress," *Psychology Today*, March 6, 2019.

Page 87 **"taking paternity leave can still be perceived as weak."** Brittany Levine Beckman, "The New Dad," *Mashable*, n.d.

Page 88 **"I'm gender nonconforming."** Beth Desmond, "How Gender Fluidity Went Mainstream," *New Statesman*, June 12, 2019.

Page 88 **"gender-neutral choice of X."** Amy Harmon, "Which Box Do You Check? Some States Are Offering a Nonbinary Option," *New York Times*, May 29, 2019.

Page 88 **"first male spokesmodel."** Jake Woolf, "The New Face of Covergirl Is a Guy," *GQ*, October 12, 2016.

Page 88 **"Chanel released Boy de Chanel."** Teo Van den Broeke. "GQ's Verdict on Boy De Chanel," *GQ*, December 18, 2018.

Page 89 **"men's personal care market is expected to reach $166 billion."** Yogita Sharma, "Men's Personal Care Market to Reach $166 Billion, Globally, by 2022," press release, Allied Market Research, n.d.

Page 89 **"smash hit."** Neda Ulaby, "Girls' Legos Are a Hit? But Why Do Girls Need Special Legos?" npr.com, June 29, 2013.

Page 89 **"gender doesn't define a person."** Shepherd Laughlin, "Study: Generation Z and Gender," JWT Intelligence, May 20, 2015.

CHAPTER 6—INSTANT KNOWLEDGE

Page 93 **"brain symmetries in primates."** William Hopkins, "Evolution of Behavioral and Brain Symmetries in Primates," YouTube, December 8, 2011.

Page 94 **"the average cost for a single year."** Venessa Wong, "In 18 Years, a College Degree Could Cost about $500,00," *Buzzfeed News*, March 17, 2017.

Page 94 **"costs of higher education soar."** Michael B. Sauter, "Here's the Average Cost of College Tuition Every Year since 1971," *USA Today*, May 18, 2019.

Page 94 **"increased spending on athletics."** Kevin Kiley, "Playing Different Games," *Inside Higher Ed.*, January 16, 2013.

Page 94 Kevin Carey, *End of College: Creating the Future of Learning and University of Everywhere* (New York: Riverhead Books, 2015).

Page 95 **"trade and vocational schools."** Douglas Belkin, "Why an Honors Student Wants to Skip College and Go to Trade School," *Wall Street Journal*, March 5, 2018.

Page 95 **"Tech School 42."** "Vivienne Walt, "Radical Programming School '42' Still Solving for the Skills Gap," *Fortune*, March 16, 2019.

Page 95 **"60-year curriculum."** Alina Tugend, "60 Years of Higher Ed—Really?" *New York Times*, October 10, 2019.

Page 95 **"slacker culture."** Mike McPadden, "25 Years of 'Slacker' and the Quarter Century of Indie Cred It Spawned," *Kindland*, August 1, 2016.

Page 96 **"Time-Starved Doer."** http://www.nonobvious.com/guides.

Page 96 **"Fender Play."** Amy X. Wang, "Fender Is Expanding Its Audience through More Than Just Guitars," *Rolling Stone*, October 18, 2018.

Page 96 **"half a billion views."** April Glaser, "How BuzzFeed Makes Money from Its Tasty Food Videos," *Vox*, February 15, 2017.

Page 96 **"hip-hop songs about school subjects."** Nigel Roberts, "Hip-Hop Edtech Company Challenges Traditional Teaching Flow," *NewsOne*, February 27, 2017.

Page 97 **"online master classes."** David S. Rudin, "The Idea That Successful People Can Teach Their Secrets Isn't New. Now MasterClass Is Selling It for $180," *Vox*, January 16, 2019.

Page 97 **"plumbing and heating industry."** Robert Waters, "Virtual Reality: A New Frontier for HVAC Training," hpacmag.com, February 23, 2018.

Page 97 "medical industry." Andrew Zaleski, "Virtual Reality Gets Real in the Operating Room, ," *Fortune*, January 9, 2019.

Page 97 "virtual reality training modules." "UPS Enhances Driver Safety Training with Virtual Reality," press release, UPS, June 6, 2019.

Page 97 "learn something more slowly." Project Zero, a group founded at the Harvard Graduate School of Education, has studied this effect of slow learning and how "learning is a consequence of thinking" for more than four decades.

Page 98 "endangered at some level." Nina Strochlic, "The Race to Save the World's Disappearing Languages, "*National Geographic*, April 16, 2018.

Page 98 before their last living speaker dies." Strochlic, "The Race to Save the World's Disappearing Languages."

Page 98 "knowledge of edible and medicinal foods." George Dvorsky, "Here Are Some Essential Skills We've Lost from Our Ancient Ancestors," *Gizmodo*, September 23, 2015.

Page 98 "weaker grip strength." Natalie Jacewicz, "Millennials May Be Losing Their Grip," npr.com, June 13, 2016.

Page 99 "guy on a Jet Ski." Nicholas Carr, *The Shallows: What the Internet Is Doing to Our Brains* (New York: Norton, 2011).

Page 99 "passive haptic learning." Thad Starner and Caitlyn Seim, "Passive Haptic Learning: Learn to Type or Play Piano without Attention Using Wearables," Georgia Tech GVU Center, n.d.

Page 99 "Neuralink." Ashlee Vance, "Elon Musk's Neuralink Says It's Ready for Brain Surgery," *Bloomberg Busdisnessweek*, July 17, 2019.

Page 99 "higher cognitive abilities." "Penn Study Finds Gray Matter Increases during Adolescence," *Penn Medicine News*, May 26, 2017.

Page 99 "gray matter density in bilingual people." "Bilinguals of Two Spoken Languages Have More Gray Matter Than Monolinguals," news release, Georgetown University Medical Center, July 16, 2015.

Page 99 "students . . . watch videos at a faster pace." Clive Thompson, "If You Want to Learn Faster, Overclock Your Audio and Video," *Wired*, February 11, 2017.

Page 99 "one recent study." Raymond Pastore and Albert D. Ritzhaupt, "Using Time-Compression to Make Multimedia Learning More Efficient: Current Research and Practice," *TechTrends* 59, no. 2 (2015): 66–74.

CHAPTER 7—REVIVALISM

Page 103 The Office "Local Ad" (Episode Highlight) YouTube, October 20, 2017.

Page 103 "Newsweek goes digital only." Jennifer Saba, Peter Lauria, "After 79 years in print, Newsweek goes digital only," *Newsweek*, October 18, 2012.

Page 103 "sales of physical books are expected to grow." *PwC's Global Entertainment & Media Outlook 2018-2022*

Page 103 "fondness for physical books." Ellen Duffer, "Readers Still Prefer Physical Books," *Forbes*, May 28, 2019

Page 104 "younger people prefer texting." Bill Murphy Jr. "Millennials and Gen Z Would Rather Text Each Other Than Do This, According to a New Study," *Forbes*, October 26, 2017

Page 104 "Why the notebook is flourishing." Josephine Wolff, "Why the Humble Notebook Is Flourishing in the iPhone Era," *The New Republic*, June 21, 2016.

Page 105 "Online art auctions." Elisabeth Kiefer, "These online galleries are helping millennials become art collectors," *The Washington Post*, July 24, 2018.

Page 105 "Board games are back." Don Jolin, "The rise and rise of tabletop gaming," *The Observer*, September 25, 2016.

Page 105 "The right to repair our things." Bob Garfield, "The Right to Repair Our Things," *On the Media*, May 22, 2015.

Page 105 "Why the Boeing Max 737 crashed twice." Vox, "The real reason Boeing's new plane crashed twice," YouTube, April 15, 2019.

Page 105 "Growing sales of 'dumb phones.'" Shobhit Srivastava, "Global Smartphone Shipments Reached Record 1.55 Billion Units in CY 2017," *Counterpoint*, February 2, 2018.

Page 105 "Why people prefer dumb phones." Rachel Hosie, "'Dumbphone' Sales Rise as People Seek to Disconnect and Be More Mindful," *Independent*, August 20, 2018.

Page 106 **"Abandoning wearable fitness trackers."** Sara Kessler, "Wearables With Style?," *FastCompany*, November 14, 2014.

Page 106 **"Hacking election machines."** Mark Niesse, "How to hack elections on Georgia's electronic voting machines," *The Atlanta Journal-Constitution*, April 18, 2018.

Page 106 **"election hacking concern."** Alejandro de la Garza, "Should You Be Afraid of Election Hacking? Here's What Experts Say," Time, October 25, 2018.

Page 106 **"proof of Russian interference."** Dustin Volz and Alan Cullison, "'Putin Has Won': Mueller Report Details the Ways Russia Interfered in the 2016 Election," *The Wall Street Journal*, April 19, 2019.

Page 106 **"Voting moves back to paper ballots."** Alejandro de la Garza, "Should You Be Afraid of Election Hacking? Here's What Experts Say," Time, October 25, 2018.

Page 106 **Kodak ad.** Kosmo Foto, September 20, 2019.

Page 107 **"Kodak declares bankruptcy."** Michael J. de la Merced, "Eastman Kodak Files for Bankruptcy," *Dealbook*, January 19, 2012.

Page 107 **"How Kodak failed."** Chunka Mui, "How Kodak Failed," *Forbes*, January 18, 2019.

Page 107 **"Steve Sasson invents digital camera."** David Gann, "Kodak invented the digital camera - then killed it. Why innovation often fails," *World Economic Forum*, Jun 23, 2016.

Page 107 **"Fall of Kodak—by the numbers."** "The rise and fall of Kodak: By the numbers," October 3, 2011.

Page 107 **"Iconic Super 8 camera."** Remy Melina, "What Happened to Super 8 Film, and Why Was It So Great?," *Live Science*, June 8, 2011.

Page 107 **"Kodachrome magazine."** "Kodak's Magazine Kodachrome Celebrates All Things Print," April 23, 2018

Page 107 **"Kodak launches branded clothing."** Kaitlyn Tiffany, "Kodak wants to resurrect itself. So it's looking to analog-obsessed teens," *Vox*, September 13, 2018.

Page 107 **"Arcade bars in Buenos Aires."** Valentin Muro, "When Arcade Games Meet Hipster Bars: The Resurgence of '80s Culture in Buenos Aires," *Culture Trip*, July 9, 2018.

Page 107 **"Edmonton arcade bars."** Margeaux Maron, "The competition heats up: pair of new arcade bars open in Edmonton Friday," *Global News*, September 19, 2019.

Page 107 **"Video game sales break $43.8B in 2018."** "U.S. Video Game Sales Reach Record-Breaking $43.4 Billion in 2018," January 22, 2019.

Page 107 **"Rise of retro gaming."** Jake Rossen, "Bit by Bit: Inside the Rise of Retro Gaming," *MF*, September 26, 2017.

Page 108 **"Film franchises continue."** Paul Glynn, "The Matrix: How have other 'fourth' films fared?," bbc.com, August 21, 2019.

Page 108 **"Sir Patrick Stewart agrees to play Jean-Luc Picard again."** Aaron Couch and Lesly Goldberg, "'Star Trek' Boss: Picard Leads "Radically Altered" Life in CBS All Access Series," The Hollywood Reporter, January 8, 2019.

Page 108 **"Talarico umbrellas."** Ann Hood, "In the Quest for Italy's Rain Man," *National Geographic Traveller India*, August 9, 2018.

Page 109 **"Kari Voutilainen watchmaker."** Simon de Burton, "Kari Voutilainen and Watchmaking by Hand," *The New York Times*, March 22, 2018.

Page 110 **"preserve their memory."** Tom Cheshire, "Archaeology's future lies in 3D scanning the past," *WIRED UK*, January 8, 2016.

Page 110 **"easier to experience."** Geraldine Fabrikant, "Preserving the Past for Museum Visitors of the Future," *New York Times*, October 23, 2019.

Page 110 **"access on demand."** Meredith Shifman, "My Travels With Pinchas Gutter," Museum of Jewish Heritage blog, September 26, 2017.

CHAPTER 8—HUMAN MODE

Page 113 **"$16.4 billion."** These figures are from publicly filed 2019 reports: the Uniform Application for Investment Adviser Registration and Report by Exempt Reporting Advisers.

Page 113 **"it added a human option."** John Detrixhe, "Financial Robo-Advisers Are Finding That a Little Human Touch Goes a Long Way," *Quartz*, July 26, 2017.

Page 114 **"report from McKinsey."** Michael Chui, James Manyika, and Mehdi Miremadi, "Where Machines Could Replace Humans—and Where They Can't (Yet)," *McKinsey Digital*, n.d.

Page 114 **"coolest brand in America."** Robert Klara, "How Shinola Went from Shoe Polish to the Coolest Brand in America," *AdWeek*, June 22, 2015.

Page 115 **"Shinola's origin story."** Stacy Perman, "The Real History of America's Most Authentic Fake Brand," *Inc.*, n.d.

Page 115 **"Korean *mukbang*."** Elise Hu, "Koreans Have an Insatiable Appetite for Watching Strangers Binge Eat," npr.com, March 24, 2015.

Page 116 **"Please Don't Kill Yourself."** Anna Akana, "Please Don't Kill Yourself," YouTube, September 27, 2013.

Page 116 **"by posing partially nude."** Amy Schumer, "Beautiful, Gross, Strong, Thin, Fat, Pretty, Ugly, Sexy, Disgusting, Flawless, Woman," Twitter, November 30, 2015.

Page 116 **"a model with vitiligo."** Katie O'Malley, "Winnie Harlow Proudly Shows Off Her Vitiligo in Stunning Body-Positive Selfie," *Elle*, August 17, 2017.

Page 116 **"avoid excessive picture retouching."** Megan Gibson, "One Fashion Brand Takes the 'No Photoshop Pledge.' Who's Next?" *Time*, August 19, 2014.

Page 116 **"relaxed checkout."** "Tesco in Forres Introduces 'Relaxed' Lane," bbc.com, January 18, 2017.

Page 117 **"'sign-language only' location."** Adia H. Robinson, "A Starbucks Opens Its First 'Signing Store' for the Deaf and Hard of Hearing in DC Today," *Washingtonian*, October 23, 2018.

Page 117 **"hire more neurodiverse."** Vauhini Vara, "Microsoft Wants Autistic Coders. Can It Find Them and Keep Them?" *Fast Company*, September 6, 2016.

Page 117 **"Tommy Adaptive."** Makita Rivas, "Tommy Hilfiger Releases Their Spring 2018 Adaptive Collection Campaign," *Teen Vogue*, April 4, 2018.

Page 117 **"*1,000 Cut Journey*."** "'1000 Cut Journey' Launches at Tribeca Film Festival," Brown Institute, Columbia University, April 26, 2018.

Page 118 **"prisoner in solitary confinement."** "Welcome to Your Cell," *Guardian Weekly*, n.d.

Page 118 **"world's greatest empathy machine."** Chris Milk, "How Virtual Reality Can Create the Ultimate Empathy Machine," *TED2015*, March 2015.

Page 118 **"truck drivers."** Trip Gabriel, "Alone on the Open Road: Truckers Feel Like 'Throwaway People,'" *New York Times*, May 22, 2017.

Page 118 **"female prisoners."** Shiho Fukada, "Japan's Prisons Are a Haven for Elderly Women," *Bloomberg Businessweek*, March 16, 2018.

Page 119 **"older people are projected to outnumber children."** "Older People Projected to Outnumber Children for the First Time in U.S. History," press release, U.S. Census, March 13, 2018.

Page 119 **"prefer to age at home."** Danielle Arigoni, "Preparing for an Aging Population," *AARP Livable Communities*, May 2018.

Page 119 **"like the loss of a family member."** "They Welcomed a Robot into Their Family; Now They're Mourning Its Death," *Verge*, June 19, 2019.

CHAPTER 9—ATTENTION WEALTH

Page 125 **"always missing out."** Rohit Bhargava, "The Reality of Always Missing Out," medium.com, n.d.

Page 126 **"attention spans are getting shorter."** Kevin McSpadden, "You Now Have a Shorter Attention Span Than a Goldfish," *Time*, May 14, 2015.

Page 126 **"Flugtag."** See the Red Bull website: www.redbullflugtagusa.com.

Page 127 **"Museum of Agriculture . . . and Cheetos Museum."** Kristina Monllos, "Why Brands Are Building Their Own 'Museums,' Where Immersion Is the Price of Entry," *AdWeek*, August 7, 2016.

Page 127 **"'sugary spectacle.'"** See https://www.showclix.com/event/candytopia-san-fransisco.

Page 128 **"MartinPatrick3."** Jahna Pelquin, "North Loop Men's Shop MartinPatrick3 Planning Another Expansion," *Star Tribune*, June 15, 2018.

Page 128 **"just-looking fee."** Amanda Kooser, "Store Charges $5 'Showrooming' Fee to Looky-Loos," cnet.com, March 26, 2013.

Page 128 **"Toys 'R' Us announced."** "Toys 'R' Us Announces First New Stores, But You Might Not Recognize Them," *Forbes*, July 18, 2019.

Page 128 **"Olympics-branded phones."** "Samsung Delivers 12,500 Galaxy S7 Edge Olympic Games Limited Edition Phones to Rio 2016 Olympians," press release, Samsung, August 4, 2016.

Page 128 **"Dreamery in New York."** See the Dreamery website: https://dreamerybycasper.com/.

Page 129 **"Stories are a powerful tool."** Paul J. Zak, "Why Your Brain Loves Good Storytelling," *Harvard Business Review*, October 28, 2014.

Page 129 **"'everyone's beauty BFF.'"** Sneha Mankani, "Huda Kattan Spills the Beans on How She Built Her Beauty Empire," *Vogue*, September 7, 2017.

Page 129 **"internet's most influential people."** "The 26 Most Influential People on the Internet," *Time*, June 26, 2017.

Page 129 **"52 acquisitions."** Stephanie Holi-Nga Wong, "The Latest Acquisition Targets Are Indie Beauty Brands," *Bloomberg Businessweek*, March 23, 2017.

Page 130 **"Hatsune Miku."** Charles Poladian, "Japanese Pop Star Hatsune Miku Is Taking Over America—Never Mind That She's Not Human," *International Business Times*, June 1, 2016.

Page 130 **"'digital supermodel' created by Cameron-James Wilson."** Aida Alti, "Interview with Cameron-James Wilson, Creator of Shudu, 'The World's First Digital Supermodel,'" wersm.cop, December 10, 2018.

Page 130 **"controversial Calvin Klein ad."** Nicole Sanders, "Bella Hadid Makes Out with Lil Miquela in Calvin Klein Campaign," *Harpers Bazaar*, May 16, 2019.

Page 131 **"sabotaging her chances."** Shibani Mahtani and Regine Cabato, "Why Crafty Internet Trolls in the Philippines May Be Coming to a Website Near You," *Washington Post*, July 25, 2019.

page xx 131 x **"shake our belief in what is real."** Rob Price, "Researchers Taught AI to Write Totally Believable Fake Reviews, and the Implications Are Terrifying," *Business Insider*, August 29, 2017.

Page 131 **"*New York Times* reported the single biggest surge."** Matthew J. Belvedere and Michael Newberg, "New York Times Subscription Growth Soars Tenfold, Adding 132,000, after Trump's Win," cnbc.com, November 29, 2016.

Page 132 **"highest-rated quarter."** Joe Otterson, "Cable News Ratings: MSNBC, CNN, Fox News Post Double-Digit Growth in Q2," *Variety*, June 27, 2017.

Page 132 **"'outrage porn.'"** Eric Sasson, "The Liberal Response to Trump Is Devolving into Outrage Porn," *New Republic*, November 25, 2016.

Page 132 **"Every 'breaking' news alert."** David Weigel, "How 'Breaking News' Broke the News," *Slate*, April 20, 2012.

Page 132 **"serious commercial consequences."** Tim Wu, *The Attention Merchants* (New York: Knopf, 2016), 23

Page 133 **"reaches an audience of more than 7 million subscribers."** Peter Kafka, "TheSkimm Is Raising $12 Million from Google Ventures and Other Investors to Build Its Subscription Basis," vox.com. March 15, 2018.

Page 134 **"'online echo chamber.'"** Natasha Singer, "The Trouble with the Echo Chamber Online," *New York Times*, May 28, 2011.

CHAPTER 10—PURPOSEFUL PROFIT

Page 139 **"doing the right thing."** Yvon Chouinard, "The Next Hundred Years," presented at the Design of Prosperity 09, University of Boras, November 2, 1995.

Page 139 **"allowing customers to trade in used gear."** Footprint Chronicles, n.d., https://www .patagonia.com/footprint.html.

Page 140 **"brand's mission statement."** Emily Stifler Wolfe, "Patagonia Founder Yvon Chouinard Is in Business to Save the Earth—Not Wall Street," *Esquire*, April 24, 2019.

Page 140 **"social impact rather than growth."** Lindsay Blakely, "Patagonia's Unapologetically Political Strategy and the Massive Business It Has Built," *Inc.*, November 30, 2018.

Page 140 **"blood diamonds."** Aryn Baker, "Blood Diamonds," *Time*, n.d. https://time.com/blood-diamonds/.

Page 140 **"dangers of sugar and high-fructose corn syrup."** Katherine Zeratsky, "What Is High-Fructose Corn Syrup? What Are the Health Concerns?" Mayo Clinic, n.d.

Page 141 **"CosmEthics."** "CosmEthics Unveils the Truth behind Beauty Products," *Helsinki Smart Region*, n.d.

Page 141 **"Aspiration Bank."** Andrei Cherny, "Meet AIM: The Aspiration Impact Measurement," *Aspiration* (blog), April 26, 2018.

Page 141 **"credit card with a carbon limit."** Adele Peters, "This Credit Car Won't Let You Buy Anything Else after You've Hit Your Annual Carbon Limit," *Fast Company*, May 6, 2019.

Page 141 **"voting with your wallet."** Melanie Curtin, "Seventy-Three Percent of Millennials Are Willing to Spend More Money on This One Type of Product," *Inc.*, March 20, 2018.

Page 141 "Greta Thunberg, whose silent protests." Masha Gessen, "The Fifteen-Year-Old Climate Activist Who Is Demanding a New Kind of Politics," *New Yorker*, October 2, 2018.

Page 142 "to be more transparent." Dan Tynan, "Why Brands Are under Increasing Pressure to Be Transparent about What They Believe In," *AdWeek*, April 15, 2018.

Page 142 "war against the plastic straw." Brenna Houck, "How the Plastic Straw Ban Became the Biggest Trend of 2018," *Eater*, December 27, 2018.

Page 142 "growth in socially responsible investments." Emily Chasan, "Global Sustai nable Investments Rise 34 Percent Investments Rise to $30.7 Million," bloomberg.com, April 1, 2019.

Page 142 "millennials are twice as likely." "Millennials Drive Growth in Sustainable Investing," Morgan Stanley, August 7, 2017.

Page 142 "CVS ... converted stores to become 'health hubs.'" Nathan Bomey, "How Quitting Tobacco Reshaped CVS: Q&A with CEO Larry Merlo," *USA Today*, September 3, 2019.

Page 143 "plant-based plastic." See https://www.lego.com/en-us/aboutus/news-room/2018/march/pfp.

Page 143 "intentions to go fur-free." Oliver Franklin-Watts, "Stella McCartney Is on a Quest to Save You from the Fashion Industry," *Wired*, December 6, 2018.

Page 144 "Stony Creek Colors." Amy Feldman, "Stony Creek Colors Is Convincing Tobacco Farmers to Grow Indigo, Building a Business on Natural Dyes," *Forbes*, August 17, 2017.

Page 145 "Ocean Cleanup project." Michel Martin and Amanda Morris, "An Engineering Wunderkind's Ocean Plastics Cleanup Device Hits a Setback," npr.com, January 5, 2019.

Page 145 "ten times better." Tony Schwartz, "Companies that Practice 'Conscious Capitalism' Perform 10x Better," *Harvard Business Review*, April 4, 2013.

Page 145 Dr. Eliza Shah and Paresh Shah: In addition to being the authors of the forthcoming book *Lifters*, both authors have partnered with Non-Obvious Company, a venture started by the author of this book. See www.iamalifter.com.

CHAPTER 11—DATA ABUNDANCE

Page 151 "what gets measured . . ." *The Practice of Management*, Peter Drucker, 1954.

Page 152 "facial tracking ban." Video, producer Aubrey Patti, "Why Some Cities Are Banning Facial Recognition Technology," *WIRED*, August 8, 2019.

Page 152 "data that currently exists ... multiply exponentially." Daniel Zeichner, "The big data explosion sets us profound challenges - how can we keep up?," *The Guardian*, July 2, 2016.

Page 153 "Farmer's Business Network." Alex Konrad, "How Farmers Business Network Plans To Disrupt Big Agra, One Farm At A Time," *Forbes*, March 7, 2017.

Page 153 "Instagram for doctors." Steven Melendez, "How Figure 1, The "Instagram For Doctors" App, Plans To Introduce AI," *FastCompany*, June 14, 2017.

Page 153 "GovLab Index." The GovLab Index, GovLab.com

Page 155 "fake accounts." Vanessa Romo, "Facebook Removed Nearly 3.4 Billion Fake Accounts In 6 Months," npr.com, May 23,2019.

Page 155 "lack of quality measurement." Lauren Johnson, "When Procter & Gamble Cut $200 Million in Digital Ad Spend, It Increased Its Reach 10%," *AdWeek*, March 1, 2018.

Page 156 "curating their accounts." Jessica Contrera, "13, right now," *The Washington Post*, May 25, 2016.

Page 156 "hide likes." MIX, "Instagram is hiding likes in 6 more countries so you can post like no one's watching," thenextweb.com, July 18, 2019.

Page 156 "wearable fitness tracker growth." Alicia Phaneuf, "Latest trends in medical monitoring devices and wearable health technology," *Business Insider*, July 19, 2019.

Page 157 "self-recorded health information." Fred N. Pelzman, MD., "Doctors and patients are drowning in data. What can be done about it?, KevinMD.com, December 30, 2017.

Page 158 "Ping An." Shu-Ching Jean Chen, "Chinese Giant Ping An Looks Beyond Insurance To A Fintech Future," *Forbes*, June 6, 2017.

page 159 "benefit immediacy." Will Rinehart, "The Law & Economics of "Owning Your Data"," *American Action Forum*, April 18, 2018.

Page 159 "social credit system." Alexandra Ma, "China has started ranking citizens with a creepy 'social credit' system — here's what you can do wrong, and the embarrassing, demeaning ways they can punish you," *Business Insider*, October 29, 2018.

Page 159 "worst case scenarios." Louise Matsakis, "How the West Got China's Social Credit System Wrong," *WIRED*, July 29, 2019.

CHAPTER 12—PROTECTIVE TECH

Page 164 "AI chatbot 'therapist.'" Megan Molteni, "The Chatbot Therapist Will See You Now," *Wired*, June 7, 2017.

Page 165 "even save lives." Diana Kwon, "Can Facebook's Machine-Learning Algorithms Accurately Predict Suicide?" *Scientific American*, March 8, 2017.

Page 165 "risk of becoming problem gamblers." Dirk Hanson, "Can Gambling Machines Prevent Addiction?" *Scientific American*, November 1, 2013.

Page 165 "diagnose Parkinson's disease through facial recognition." Erin Smith, "Episode 25: Meet the High School Student Who Is Changing Parkinson's Disease Diagnosis," *The Parkinson's Foundation podcast*, March 27, 2018.

Page 165 "candy-denying vending machine." Jenn Harriss, "This Vending Machine Can Use Facial Recognition to Deny You Junk Food," *Los Angeles Times*, December 10, 2014.

Page 166 "world of service bots." Khari Johnson, "Delivery Robot Company Savioke Raises $13.4 Million to Expand into Hospitals," *VentureBeat*, June 28, 2018.

Page 166 "'smartest building in the world.'" Tom Randall, "The Smartest Building in the World," *Bloomberg Businessweek*, September 23, 2015.

Page 167 "BroApp." John Brownlee, "BroApp Sends Texts to Your GF, So You Can Spend More Time with Your Bros," *Fast Company*, February 27, 2014.

Page 167 "drones to police the wilderness". Rachel Nuwer, "High Above, Drones Keep Watchful Eyes on Wildlife in Africa," *New York Times*, March 13, 2017.

Page 168 "process for manipulating the weather." Trevor Nace, "China Is Launching Weather-Control Machines across an Area the Size of Alaska," *Forbes*, May 10, 2018.

Page 168 "prevent rain on their wedding day." Uma Sharma and Alyssa Pagano, "Here's How We'll Control the Weather in 100 Years," *Business Insider*, July 19, 2019.

Page 169 "Estonians are pioneers of digital identifiers." Vivienna Walt, "Is This Tiny European Nation a Preview of Our Tech Future"? *Fortune*, April 27, 2017.

Page 169 "protecting [governments] from cyberattacks." Lilsa Past and Keith Brown, "Attacks against Elections Are Inevitable—Estonia Shows What Can Be Done," *The Conversation*, March 28, 2019.

Page 169 "Chaos Computer Club." Jose Miguel Calatayud, "Chaos Computer Club: How Did Computer 'Freaks' in Germany Come Together?" political critique.org, January 8, 2019.

Page 170 "prevent electoral hacking." Tom Burt, "ElectionGuard available today to enable secure, verifiable voting." Microsoft Press release, September 24, 2019.

Page 170 "DoNotPay app." James Titcomb, "British 22-Year-Old's 'Robot Lawyer' App Raises $4.6m from Facebook Backers," *Telegraph*, July 4, 2019.

Page 170 "free virtual credit card." Emily Dreyfuss, "This Clever New Service Auto-Cancels Your Free Trials," *Wired*, July 17, 2018.

Page 172 "devolved into a 'racist asshole.'" James Vincent, "Twitter Taught Microsoft's AI Chatbot to Be a Racist Asshole in Less Than a Day," *Verge*, May 24, 2016.

CHAPTER 13—FLUX COMMERCE

Page 173 "Spanish theater tax." Fiona Govan, "Spain abandons the theatre," The Guardian, March 26, 2013.

Page 173 "high priced carrots." Lauren Frayer, "To Get Around Tax Hike, Spanish Theater Sells Carrots, Not Tickets," npr.org, November 12, 2012.

Page 173 "pay per laugh." Watch the full promo video for this campaign here: https://vimeo.com/97413457

Page 174 "mattress sales boom online." Rick Romell, "Online sales boom for mattresses squished into boxes," *Milwaukee Journal Sentinel*, May 8, 2017.

Page 174 "Red Bull media empire." Duff McDonald, "Red Bull's billionaire maniac becomes a media mogul," *Bloomberg Businessweek*, May 22, 2011.

Page 175 "15 sports teams across 11 sports." Sam Few, "The Red Bull sporting dynasty: From football to F1 teams—all you need to know," *Mirror*, February 23, 2019.

Page 175 "major content provider"

Page 175 "human and friendly banking experience." Jeffrey Pilcher, "Capital One Cafés: Coffee Shops or Bank Branches?," *The Financial Brand*, n.d.

Page 175 "Taco Bell hotel." Sherry Barkas, "Taco Bell's pop-up hotel reservations sell out in 2 minutes," *Palm Springs Desert Sun*, June 28, 2019.

Page 175 "largest agency companies in the world." E.J. Schultz, "The Race—How IBM, Accenture, PwC and Deloitte Are Shaking Up the Marketing Industry," *AdAge*, May 2, 2017.

Page 175 "custom content studios." Max Willens, "Publishers are expanding their content studios to do more agency work," *Digiday*, October 4, 2018.

Page 175 "Amazon enters grocery market." Barbara Kah and Mark Cohen, "Can Amazon Reinvent the Traditional Supermarket?," *Knowledge@Wharton*, March 21, 2019.

Page 176 "drop-off in car ownership." Partner Collaborators, "Demographic Shifts: Shaping the Future of Car Ownership," *Knowledge@Wharton*, February 21, 2017.

Page 177 "on-demand divorce legal services." Jeff Bercovici, "This Company Is Making Divorce Less Painful," *Inc*, October 2015.

Page 177 "Pared connects restaurants." Kate Krader, "Restaurants Are Using An App to Staff Their Kitchens," *Bloomberg Businessweek*, April 18, 2019.

Page 177 "Uber Works." John Pletz, "Uber launches staffing business in Chicago," *Crain's Chicago Business*, October 2, 2019.

Page 177 "CargoX." Alex Konrad, "How Brazil's 'Uber For Trucks' Quietly Reached A $200 Million Run Rate In Just Six Years," *Forbes*, March 9, 2018.

Page 177 "warehouse space on demand." Patrick Sisson, "On-demand warehouses power today's hip consumer brands," *Curbed*, May 24, 2019.

Page 177 "restaurant co-working space." Nellie Bowles, "Sorry, Power-Lunchers. This Restaurant Is a Co-Working Space Now," *New York Times*, July 8, 2018.

Page 177 "retail apocalypse." Vox staff, "The retail apocalypse: traditional retail chains are dying across America," *Vox*, April 1, 2019.

Page 177 "smart mirrors." Sabrina Sandalo, "Smart Mirrors Transform Retail," *Antedote*, n.d.

Page 177 "nearables." Amy Webb, "How Nearables Will Change Your Business," *Inc*, September 2015.

Page 178 "home improvement stores ..." Suman Bhattacharyya, "Lowe's is using VR and AR to get people into stores," *Digiday*, July 25, 2018.

Page 178 "invisible checkout." Sophia Kunthara, "Skip the checkout: Cashier-free tech on the rise ," *San Francisco Chronicle*, December 16, 2018.

Page 178 "dynamic pricing." Jerry Useem, "How Online Shopping Makes Suckers of Us All," *The Atlantic*, May 2017.

Page 178 "price colluding bots." Editors, "Price-bots can collude against consumers," *The Economist*, May 6, 2017.

INDEX

Current trends are in **Bold**. Trends from previous years are in *Italics*.

Trend workshop, 64–66
 adopting a "yes, and"
   mindset in, 65
 capture first, critique later
   in, 64–65
 having an unbiased
   facilitator in, 65–66
 preparing for, 64
Trump, Donald
 decline in racial prejudice
   under, 77
 2016 victory of, 131
Truthing (2018), 133, 137, 220, 221
Twists, going for, 42

U

Uber, 159, 176
Uber Works, 177
Ubiquitous Addiction, 47
Unbiased facilitators, 65–66
Unfamiliar, wandering into the,
 54–55
Ungendered (2018), 92, 221
Ungendered consumption,
 88–89
Ungendering, 81–92
 evolution of, 92
 femininity movement and,
   83–84
 gender x and, 88
 at a glance, 90
 male confusion and, 86–87
 muddled masculinity and,
   84–86
 testosterone as overrated
   and, 87
 ungendered consumption
   and, 88–89

using, 91
Unperfection (2015), 42, 115,
 208, 211
Unperfection, praise of,
 115–116
Unusual, saving of the, 31
Usership, 176–177

V

Values, being vocal about,
 141–142
Van Ness, Jonathan, 88
Variety, focusing on, 45
Versace, 144
Vertical industries, 175
Vinyl records, 104
Virtual credit cards, 168
Virtual Empathy (2016 +2018),
 40, 117–118, 122, 212, 215,
 222
Virtual reality, 40, 97
Visualized Data (2011), 194
Vocal, being about values,
 141–142
Vocational schools, 95
Voice-enabled devices, 151
Volvo, 176
Vonnegut, Kurt, 6
Voutilainen, Kari, 108–109
Vulnerability, praise of, 115–116

W

Wakefield, Elizabeth, 84
Wakefield, Jessica, 84
Wall Street Journal, 175
Wangda (social outcast), 71
Warby Parker, 128
Wealth, attention, 125–137

Wearable fitness trackers,
 156–157, 163
Weisberg, Danielle, 133
West Elm, 175
Wevorce, 177
White hat hackers, 167–168
Whole Foods, 175
Wilde, Oscar, 50
Wilson, Cameron-James, 130
Winehouse, Amy, 76
Woebot, 162
Words
 mashup, 42
 seeking out common,, in
   elevating ideas, 38
Workshops, running trend,
 64–66
World Values Survey (WVS),
 72, 77
Writing, 23. *See also* Blogs
 dialogue, 23
Wu, Tim, 132

X

Xenophobia, 77

Y

Year of Drones, 9
Yerkes National Primate
 Research Center, 93
"Yes, and Mindset," 65
YouTube, 75. 115–116, 101

Z

Zakin, Carly, 133
Zappas, 61
Zhao, Ben, 131

ROHIT BHARGAVA IS ON A MISSION to help the world be more open-minded by teaching others how to be non-obvious thinkers. He is the founder of the Non-Obvious Company and an entertaining, original and "non-boring" keynote speaker on innovation and trust. He previously spent 15 years in leadership roles at two renowned ad agencies: Leo Burnett and Ogilvy. Rohit is the *Wall Street Journal* bestselling author of six books and has been invited to deliver keynote presentations in 32 countries around the world. His insights have been used by the World Bank, NASA, Intel, Disney, Colgate, Swissotel, Coca-Cola, Schwab, Under Armour, NBC Universal, American Express and hundreds of others to win the future. Rohit is a popular Adjunct Professor of Marketing and Storytelling at Georgetown University and also writes a monthly column for GQ magazine in Brazil. He believes in listening before talking, is a lifelong lover of the Olympics and lives with his wife and two boys in the Washington DC area.

TO LEARN MORE ABOUT BOOKING THE AUTHOR FOR PRIVATE WORKSHOPS OR KEYNOTE SPEECHES, VISIT:
www.rohitbhargava.com